Listening and Communicating with Energy

Ginger Bowler

Energy Medicine
Publishing
Ozark, Missouri

Published by
Energy Medicine Publishing
Ozark, Missouri
800-240-3211

Printed in the United States of America

1st printing February 2000
2nd printing May 2000
3rd printing September 2004

ISBN: 0-9678814-0-4

Proofread by Katie Bowler

Edited by Shirley D. Bowler

Jacket design by The Printing Partners; Madison, WI

**For Hanna Kroeger, my teacher, and
Rosemary and Maurice Peter "Pete"
Bowler, my parents and teachers.**

Whenever others tell me that I remind them of
my mother, father, or Hanna, I know that I have
received the highest compliment.

Contents

Author's Acknowledgments

I learned many lessons about energy through my relationships and inter-actions with Hanna Kroeger, Bobbi Brooks, Gilda Strutz, LaRae Palo, Chris Farrugia, Cindy Johnson, Sarah Good, and many other friends, family, and teachers. These beautiful people are so tuned in that they never cease to inspire and empower me with their awareness and their goodness. I continue to learn new lessons with each passing day. There is so much to learn.

There have been many people who have helped me through the writing of this book either by reading and critiquing it, correcting it, verifying stories, or telling me when they didn't understand my meanings in various parts. To all of them, I give my thanks and appreciation. They include LaRae J. Palo, Bobbi Brooks, Dottie Bowler, Chris Farrugia, Gisela Hoffman, and the one who stuck it out with me through every page, Kathleen Roush. Also, to my editors, Katie Bowler Seal and Shirley Bowler.

I would also like to thank God and all His angels for guiding me through this project.

Foreword

One morning in 1997 (before Hanna Kroeger passed on) my partner, LaRae Palo, awoke from a prophetic dream in which she had seen the cover of a book I was going to write. She could see the cover very clearly with the title, **Listening and Communicating with Energy.** She proceeded to tell me about the dream, and then she sketched the way she had seen the title written. She also said, "At first I thought I was supposed to write it with you, but clearly you are supposed to write it alone."

This was the first time I had ever considered writing a book about the energy phenomenon since I was still a student of the subject.

Inspired by this clear message, I began to write. What did I know about energy? How had I learned about energy? The face of my beloved teacher Hanna Kroeger entered my consciousness as I thought about all that she had taught me, and was continuing to teach me, on this subject.

As I wrote, I remembered how many other people were influential in my quest to understand energy and energy fields. I became aware that this search for understanding had started during the innocence of childhood and was still a fire that burned within me.

I realized that I had an understanding of energy and energy fields and that I continue to get clearer with each passing day.

Many people see the body's energy fields or see the energy fields around plants and animals, but for the most part, I do not. At the present time, my ability seems to be more concentrated in *feeling and reading the energy fields* rather than seeing them. This *reading* is done through the use of a dowsing instrument or through intuition, when one is not able *to see* them with the physical eyes. I also see the absence or presence of light which can be a great indicator. But more of what happens with me is that I *hear* or *recognize the energy* of certain conditions in the physical and spiritual body. This I learned from Hanna Kroeger.

But what good is the ability to read energy fields and see the weaknesses in the field if you have no way to help correct these conditions? This was the power of Hanna Kroeger's teachings. She taught me about the reality of the auric energy field and the Seven Physical and Seven Spiritual Causes of All Illnesses. Once we understand cause, we can take action to correct these weaknesses or illnesses.

Chapter 1
A New Chapter Begins

Kneeling

As I knelt beside her bed and stroked her hair, I couldn't help but notice the profound shifts that were happening within my own being. I was deeply consumed with grief and yet completely empowered at the same time. I was more determined than ever to carry on her work as she had pleaded with me and with each of her many students.

I felt that I was being charged with a pulsating energy that would help to carry me through the next few critical months and later years. At the same time, I was shocked at the echo in my own heart and the deep sense of loss that will accompany me throughout the rest of my life. Again and again I took one more memorizing look at the face of my beloved teacher, Hanna Kroeger, who had just passed on a few hours earlier.

Shortly after this visitation in the tiny bedroom where her eighty-four year-old body lay, I went to work with the others who were there. We had to begin the preparations for her memorial services that would occur over the course of the rest of the week. We knew that the news of Hanna's death would bring hundreds or even thousands of people to these services because she had touched so many lives.

Prior to her passing, Hanna's body had become tired and weak. This didn't stop her from traveling everywhere, taking her message to the world. There were so many stories of healing. This devotion to God's work was the energy that kept her going.

Hanna was a tiny German woman with a thick accent and a fiery spirit. She had taught thousands of students the gracious art of self-help in the area of natural and spiritual healing. She empowered us to help ourselves and help each other. She made disease and sickness easier for us to understand and taught us effective ways to take action to keep our bodies well. She impressed upon us that we also had to keep the spirit well.

But it was even more than that. For me, she gave me God. She put the spiritual and the mystical within my reach. By her example, I learned that the true understanding of the health and healing of the physical body could not be separated from the spiritual. And that these teachings could only be learned through service, not through the mind alone.

She didn't just teach us methodology. She taught us to work—to work to help, to work to learn, to put forth the effort to grapple with and struggle for the understanding of things that were previously unknown to us.

She taught us that everything was energy and that God was the Ultimate of all energies, the Creator of all energies, the abode of all energies.

I didn't have time to think about much else beside the chores at hand, but over the next few days and weeks my heart reviewed my relationship with Hanna and all the things she had taught me. It was like watching an old movie.

I realized how well I understood many things now, especially the "energy" phenomenon which had been so elusive to me at first.

Perhaps you already have an understanding of energy and a true awareness of the different types of energy fields. Maybe it is a familiar concept. It was a familiar concept to me, or should I say a "comfortable" concept? At the time I didn't fully comprehend the far-reaching implications of this passionate quest for understanding this principle.

Now it seems that everyone is talking about "energy." But as popular as the awareness of energy seems to be getting, I believe that many of us don't have any idea of how energy affects our lives. If we did, surely we would do a better job at managing it in our own lives. If we did this, surely the world would have many happier and healthier families, people, and relationships.

Perhaps energy is to humans what water is to fish.

As I became more aware of the nature of energy, I realized that what most affects our lives is the energy that we create or perpetuate with every thought, word, and action.

Perhaps we set out deliberately to understand energy in the pursuit of a scientific or spiritual quest. But more likely, the need to understand came when our lives had shattered from some tragedy or hardship. Then we woke up and realized that we needed a better understanding of why life was turning out the way it was.

Regardless of the reason we got to this precipice, it seems to coincide with our asking the questions: *'What is the meaning of my life? Why am I alive? What is my purpose?"*

Understanding *energy* from the spiritual or mystical perspective is a personal, experiential journey of the senses—all of the senses.

It is a journey, a journey none of us seem to know we are about to take before we begin it.

My Journey Begins

It was 1986. I was in my early thirties. I did not know that I was still asleep. I had experienced somewhat of a personal awakening in the early '80s, and here I was about to do it again—only this time on a different level, into the dimension of the spirit.

At the time, I didn't experience my life as a spiritual journey, rather a personal one only. It was life, my life, a day to day experience of motion.

Life was actually rather exciting on this personal level, and I was relatively happy. Life was predictable, much of the same routine, day after day.

Now I was going to get the opportunity to discover how truly unaware I was. I would actually be startled into the realization of how my ego had run my life and was going to completely use it up, had not a divine intervention been in the plans.

When a Loved One Gets Sick, God Gets Your Attention

At two-and-a-half years of age, my niece was covered with tumor-like cysts all over her body. What could cause something like that? Worse yet, what would happen to her?

My sister and brother-in-law had taken her to many doctors, specialists, and practitioners—even to an herbalist. But no one could help. The doctors couldn't even diagnose the condition.

When I saw the tumors all over her little body, my mind went to that place no mind should ever go—to despair and thinking the worst.

I was tormented with what seemed to be happening to my sweet niece. I was tortured by the fear of having to watch my sister, Maureen, lose her daughter.

By the age of four, Christy's doctors proposed removing the tumors. A little body with twenty-seven lumps removed would look like a human golf ball—not a pretty sight. But, even if they did the surgery, what would keep the tumors from coming back? Christy's twin sister Holly miraculously showed none of the same symptoms.

I didn't understand sickness or disease. I had always been interested in health and the human body. I had studied the mechanics of the body in college, but I didn't have the faintest idea what really made it work.

I asked God to forgive me for not praying when all was going well, but I was wondering if He would consider helping us, again. So many times in my life I had tried to bargain with God: *I'll give up this, if you give me that.* I don't honestly think that I ever credited this tactic for working, but I had to try it one more time.

In the ten or fifteen years preceding, I had not even thought of God or remembered to pray, except if someone died, or was going to die. So here I was again, in familiar territory, pleading and offering bargains.

I did not know if God had heard my pleas. I hoped there really was a God, one who could heal little nieces and one who would give me another chance. All I could do was pray.

And Then Came Belva

There are people in our lives who open doors for us, and only after walking through the door do we realize the significance of the role that person played. The door that was about to be opened for me altered the course of my life, forever.

I was born and raised in New Orleans, Louisiana, and was still living there at the time. I had a friend, who had a friend, who knew this woman. Her name was Belva Bloomer. Belva wasn't from New Orleans but was in the hospital there with a broken leg from a car accident.

Belva was supposed to be a spiritually progressive somebody who knew all about life: this life, the past life, the after life, the next life. In addition, she knew many famous people. She had even been a secretary for Shirley MacLaine, the famous actress, writer, and free thinker. I was enamored with famous people. I was completely fascinated. I wanted to be famous. Actually, I was determined to be famous. And I thought that if I met someone with famous people connections, I might get famous too. And then I would have met my destiny and live happily ever after.

So, I wanted to meet Belva and get the process started. I also wanted to see if she could give me some secrets about my life.

Shirley MacLaine had written a book about reincarnation. This was a topic that completely captured my interest. I felt bad for the fact that she was the brunt of ridicule by Hollywood for being so forthcoming in her beliefs about such a "way out" topic. Many people mocked her and thought she was a flake and a fanatic.

Many others were relieved that a modern, popular, normal looking person was speaking so openly on a topic that they were so interested in or were curious about.

If Belva had been around Shirley, maybe Belva knew some of what Shirley knew. Maybe Belva would even be able to introduce me to her. But if not, at the least I was sure Belva knew enough to entertain me.

I was never so excited to go to a hospital as when I was going to meet Belva. I didn't know what to expect, but I didn't expect to see someone who was supposedly so spiritual, looking just like Dolly Parton. Her broken leg was in a big cast and in traction, but she was totally made up. Her bleached blonde hair was all doodied up, and her make up was perfect and plentiful. Her eyelashes were long, and were they hers? Beautiful, unusual, odd, and intriguing. There she was, bossing the doctors around, entertaining them and anyone else who happened to be around.

Belva had a strange lilt to her voice, as though she was always laughing, even when she was serious. Somehow, everything was just a little bit funny. Somehow, everything was just completely serious.

I was not a shy person, never have been. But I felt a little shy around Belva. Somewhere in her laugh was something I had to know, had to understand. Being around her, I realized how much I didn't understand.

Have I Lived Before?

I had always been fascinated with the unknown, with mystical happenings and spiritual phenomenon.

I remember, as a young child about five years old, sitting cross-legged on the dresser staring intently at my reflection, wondering. Who am I?

As I continued to look at the little girl looking back at me, I got more upset. Where was I and who was this? I didn't know the answer to that; however, one thing I did know, was that I didn't look like the little girl in the mirror.

This was my earliest memory of thinking that I may have lived before or that there was some part of me that had lived before.

This idea was foreign, yet familiar, to me. I shoved this question aside until my friend's father, Lionel, introduced me to the idea of reincarnation. I was sixteen.

Lionel

Lionel Escudé was a beautiful, elegant, and unusual man. Lighthearted and opinionated, he had the most open mind of any man I had ever met besides my own father. He shared his belief that the soul goes through many lifetimes in an effort to learn all the different lessons it has to learn. The soul does this so that it can reach a level of perfection where it no longer requires coming back to a human life, in order to progress. In each incarnation, the soul adopts different personalities, different life circumstances, even different sexes, all so that it can learn the various lessons a perfected soul needs to learn in order to complete its journey. The purified soul is then able to reunite with God forever.

This made sense to me. It made it much easier to understand why a child might die while someone else lives to be a hundred. The lessons each soul had to *learn* or that each soul had agreed to come to *teach* required a certain amount of time in this particular incarnation. God was merciful, after all, if this was the truth.

Lionel had read most of Edgar Cayce's books and started sharing them with me. I was enthralled.

I never have gotten comfortable with the idea that some things are just mysteries that we are not meant to understand. I wanted to understand.

I searched continually for that understanding.

Belva and Christy

Actually, in a roundabout way, it was through Lionel that I met Belva. I was doing a little consulting work for Rowena LaRose, who was the soon to be sister-in-law of Lionel. Joell was Lionel's future wife and the sister of Rowena. Joell and Rowena had another sister, Betty, who was with Belva when she had the car accident that put her into the hospital. Rowena told Betty how interested I was in mystical and spiritual topics. They both knew that I would find Belva intriguing. Betty arranged for me to meet Belva.

Now that I had met Belva there was another new person in my life who could talk about these things. Belva knew so much about topics I had never even heard about. She was intriguing and believable. Her beliefs would expand my mind. She was knowledgeable and wise. She could explain some of those "mysteries." Instinctively, I knew she was telling me the "truth."

She was fun to be around, and I became the audience of a captive teacher when I went to visit her. She couldn't go anywhere. She was a "bed prisoner."

One day I wanted to talk to Belva about Christy's health crisis. I was trying to come to grips with why a four year old would have to get so sick and possibly die. The reincarnation theory wasn't bringing me much comfort because I didn't care if Christy had done something in another life requiring her to suffer and die at an early age in this one. I didn't care about Christy's past life dealings, or if she was the sacrificial lamb coming to teach us lessons by dying in this life. I didn't want any part of this karma and reincarnation theory, not now. I wanted her life spared, regardless of what I thought I knew about karma and reincarnation.

"Oh," Belva said matter-of-factly, "I know someone who can heal her."

"What? How do you mean, 'heal her'?" I questioned. "The doctors can't even diagnose it. They don't know what the problem is, but they think she will probably die from it," I said.

"It doesn't matter," Belva said. " Hanna doesn't need anybody to tell her what's wrong. She can figure it out herself. She's this little old German woman who lives in Boulder, Colorado. Her name is Hanna Kroeger. She's a real healer, completely intuitive."

Well, that's wonderful. Someone may be able to heal my niece, and she lives 1500 miles away from Louisiana. Is this good news or bad? My sister was in no position to trek across the country on the slim chance that

Belva wasn't a kook.

"A real healer, a genuinely intuitive person ... aw, man, I want to meet her," I was thinking. My fascination with all of this kicked in again. I could drive to Colorado some day. I could walk to Colorado some day. I wouldn't fly to Colorado because I was terrified to fly, but somehow, in those few moments since Belva had mentioned Hanna, I knew I had to meet her.

"Well, I'll call and ask her to come here and teach a seminar. That way your niece can have a chance to see her," Belva said.

"Really? You can do that?" I said.

"Sure," Belva said with confidence.

"Okay," I said. For some reason, this seemed sensible.

Much to the dismay of her business manager, Hanna agreed to come to New Orleans in three weeks! She had a short break in her schedule, so why not?

Getting Ready for Our First Hanna Kroeger Natural and Spiritual Healing Seminar

For the next three weeks, my friend Lee and I scurried around getting everybody we knew to come to a seminar that we knew nothing about. I didn't know too many people to ask except my family and a few openminded friends. Fortunately, Lee knew some people who would want to come to this kind of event. Better yet, she knew where all the health food stores in New Orleans were located. We would have to go to all of them to put up the advertisements once they arrived from Hanna's office in Boulder.

We were in my driveway sitting in the car when Lee opened the package that had arrived with the seminar flyers. The flyers had a nice big picture of our soon-to-be lifelong teacher, Hanna Kroeger.

Lee opened the package and then sort of swooned back and said something equally foreign to me. "The energy from these are incredible. My God!" Her body began swaying from this not so apparent energy that had somehow escaped from this packet of paper that came 1,500 miles through the mail.

"I have never felt so much energy like that from a picture. Can you feel that?" Lee continued.

"Oh, brother," I thought, "what a fruitcake!" I didn't want Lee to see me roll my eyes so I turned my head. I didn't want her to see my disbelief.

My internal dialogue continued, "No, I don't feel the energy from a piece of paper, but if you think you do, maybe you do. I doubt it, but maybe you do. But I wouldn't tell anybody else that if I were you."

In case she was right, I didn't want her to know how unenlightened I was or how out of touch I was with this energy thing, so I did not put my thoughts on external speaker.

Lee was interesting to me in many of the same ways that Belva was. But when Belva said things off the wall, I thought it was fascinating. When Lee said them, I thought she was making them up. Anyway, I was on a mission to help my niece and if I had to deal with some of this goofy *energy stuff*, okay, fine.

By this time, Belva was out of the hospital and now staying with our mutual friend, Alice. She was still fairly immobile, so while Belva orchestrated things from the bed, Lee and I hit the streets.

I didn't think that my fellow Southerners had yet heard of Hanna. Apparently some of them had. Our flyer announcing *A Natural and Spiritual Healing Seminar with Rev. Hanna Kroeger* drew a crowd, and the sweet little Unity Church that we had rented for the seminar filled up.

Chapter 2
Starting To Understand Energy

Different people had different ways of teaching me things. Lee's understanding of the reality of energy fields hadn't even been a conscious thought to me, at that point. Although, looking back, I can see many instances in my life when I was acutely aware of energy and energy fields.

Obviously it was time for me to start to understand that everything has an energy field, even photocopies. It was a stretch, but a stretch in the right direction.

As I was learning about energy in all kinds of different situations and aspects of life, I remembered learning about the pain of separation from the source of all energy.

The Walk Home

I was about ten years old. I regularly walked home from school because my participation in sports meant that I would miss the school bus. The walk wasn't too bad, long enough for reflection.

Many times on these walks home, I remember asking the questions, "When am I going to know why I came? What is the meaning of life? When am I going to find out the purpose of my life?"

Countless walks home, countless questions. Waiting, waiting, waiting. Somehow I knew that I would find out one day, when I was "grown up."

On this particular day, I wasn't questioning anything. But Pete was. My brothers, Pete and Bruce were twins, two years older than I was. Pete and Bruce came running up to me. I only had half of a block to go to get home.

"How do you know you really exist?" Pete asked pointedly. Apparently questioning runs in the family.

"How do you know you aren't dreaming your whole life up?" Pete asked again.

With a quick glance from Pete to Bruce, I knew that they were serious. This wasn't some sort of joke. They knew something I didn't. I wanted to know.

"Well, let's see," I thought. "I can figure this one out."

The twins gave me plenty of time to ponder.

"Let's see. How do I know I really exist? How do I know I am not just dreaming my life?" I repeated their question aloud. With no response from the twins but two smiling faces I had more time to consider my answer.

This was one of those rare cosmic moments in my life. By contemplating the nature of my young reality, I actually experienced my connection to all that is. I remember turning over the thought, "What if I am making this all up?"

For those few moments, I actually experienced being one with the Creator of my life.

Suddenly, things seemed different. I was experiencing something so unique, so full, so different and yet so familiar. I felt exhilarated. I experienced myself *as* everything, *with all things, one with the universe*. I was with God, of God, one with all that ever was and ever would be, and it was good. It was a magnificent few seconds. It was total. Oh, yes, what a wonderful dream. Complete. Serene. Simple. I was unaware of my limited physical surroundings and totally aware of everything. Amazing.

Out of the glow of my new found understanding I heard Pete's voice again, "Put out your hand."

So I did.

"You want me to prove to you that all of this is real?" he asked.

Since Pete was older (he was 12), he was the authority in my book. Older people knew all the secrets.

"Okay," I said.

I was glad he thought he could prove my reality. I couldn't. I was still off in the ozone somewhere.

Staring into Pete's small and serious freckled face, well, all of a sudden, I knew I wanted him to be real. I wanted my family to be real. I didn't want to wake up from this dream and discover I was alone, that I had dreamed up everybody and everything, and that there was nobody and nothing but me. That would have to mean that I was alone. Alone meant lonely. How awful that would be, I shuddered. Nobody else but me? Alone!

Suddenly, this feeling of loneliness had swallowed up my exhilaration and my feeling of connection to all things. Fear and despair replaced exuberance. The glory of my complete connection to and absorption with God disconnected.

Pete slapped my outstretched hand so hard it took my breath away. The pain resonated in my bones, in my cells, in my breath. I gasped. He smiled, triumphant and all knowing.

"Ouch!" I whimpered.

"That's how you know," he said.

"Pain," I thought. "So that's it. Pain is how we know we exist."

It was clear to me at that moment that God was real. Now I also knew that I was real. I existed, and so did Pete and Bruce. Pain is how I was sure.

My Introduction to the Healing Arts

At the age of sixteen, I had met Alice and her fascinating father, Lionel. He then led me to Edgar Cayce's work (the famous clairvoyant healer). He also took me to my first chiropractor's visit.

In the early '70s, chiropractors were considered to be "way out there" and radical. They were called quacks and were scorned by the medical profession at large. In fact, chiropractors were actually illegal in Louisiana at this time. We had to knock on a door and wait until we got the "once over" through the peephole before gaining entrance to this mystery. I thought this was exciting.

Once we entered the office, I found it felt very good to be there. It was so sweetly silent. The chiropractor was a man in his early 50s by my best guess. He had such a caring, confident manner. He could tell me things about my health just by looking at my posture and feeling my spine. I found this to be fascinating. Then he adjusted the misaligned vertebrae in my spine. The only thing I can remember him telling me to do was to drink Welch's unsweetened grape juice (room temperature with no ice). This was going to help my stomach and colon problem that still flared up from time to time.

When we were finished, we slipped out the same door we had entered and quickly walked down the street and out of sight.

This was the first of many visits in my life with people who weren't medical doctors, but who had a real understanding of health.

Early on, I had developed a total distrust for doctors. At the age of about eleven or twelve, I developed a terrible problem with my stomach and bowels. My doctor thought I was making up the problem because he couldn't find anything wrong after having sent me to have a barium enema and a G. I. series.

The stabbing cramping pains in my abdomen were real. I didn't care if it could be proven or not. The diarrhea, the sweating, the having to go to sleep for the pain to subside were all real.

One day I went to the corner drug store to pick up a prescription for this terrible, painful disorder. Prior to walking down the aisle toward the big druggist, I heard someone say that I was really just getting a sugar pill. They called it a placebo. I was a child, not an idiot. I knew what that meant. Slap, a smack, ridicule. They did not believe my pain was real, but worst of all it meant no one was going to help me.

I was embarrassed to pick up the prescription. I felt that the pharmacist was laughing at me. I now knew that the doctor thought I was faking, too. He didn't believe me. Worse, he couldn't help me. After walking out of the drug store, my embarrassment turned to anger. I would just have to learn to help myself. I would not get put in that horrible position again.

Over time, I learned to watch my own diet, to avoid greasy foods and things that would bring on an attack. I learned to suspect all medications and all doctors. If they didn't believe me, I didn't believe them. Fair trade.

From that time on, through high school and periodically in the years that followed, this same pesky problem hung on. This was the issue for which the chiropractor had told me to drink the grape juice. At one point, I did get medication that helped somewhat, but it did not help my attitude

14

toward medical doctors. I didn't want to let go of that position.

Now I was seventeen years old you know, grown up. And Lionel was showing me that there were others who knew about healing. His job in my life was obviously to start the process of opening my mind and exposing me to this other world. His world was filled with healers and intuitive people and things that I had never considered. It was filled with possibilities and hope.

He and his family took all kinds of vitamins and nutritional supplements. They seemed healthy, with slender bodies and quick minds. His family read the *Prevention* magazine, which in its early days was a radical journal. It was filled with articles on holistic health and healing combined with great information on vitamins and home remedies.

So my first magazine subscription was for the *Prevention* magazine. I started spending my baby-sitting money on mail-order vitamins from advertisements in this magazine. My family worried about me. My brother Pete told me I was going off the deep end, that I was a fanatic. They were concerned for me. I was radical at seventeen for taking vitamins!

I knew that I had to get myself educated. I instinctively knew that I was not going to find the answers I was looking for, in the world most people lived. I was going to have to look in the world that Lionel was living in.

I met Alice and Lionel during my junior year in high school. By the time I was a senior in high school, and due to my introduction to mystical phenomenon, I was clear about one goal in my life—I wanted to be like Edgar Cayce. I wanted to be psychic so that I could help people as well as myself. I thought this was the answer. I didn't know what I wanted to major in when I went to college, but I definitely wanted to be psychic.

I thought that the whole solution to problems in life was to be able to know things about the future, so that I could change the outcome wherever necessary, avoiding problems and making sure that everything was worked out perfectly.

I would later realize that the challenges in our lives are necessary for us to learn our lessons and are not to be avoided, but rather embraced. I would also come to the realization that the pursuit of psychic ability, for the sake of psychic ability, is a side trip of the ego and one that many people get lost on. Psychic ability without spiritual understanding to back it up is worth little, as far as I can tell.

But back then I would sometimes entertain new friends by telling them things about themselves that I had never been told. I found this fun.

I realized that sometimes I was more in tune than at other times, and I didn't know why. Although I seemed to have some natural intuition, as most of us do, I wasn't able to access it at will, and this bothered me.

Avoiding Death

While trying hard to understand life, I was trying even harder to avoid dealing with death.

I could deal with death in theory, as in discussing reincarnation and taking a strong position on it. But when it came time to actually accept the death of a loved one, or thinking about dying myself I was completely afraid of this orderly, sensible, consoling part of the divine plan.

As a child, I prayed that God would let my entire large family die at the same time, including me. I thought this was a great solution for not having to deal with the grief of watching your loved ones die. I wasn't sure of the purpose of my life, but I was totally sure there was no good purpose for death.

I had already had a taste of death, and I didn't like it one bit. At the age of nine, I was with my mother on her bed as she wept over the death of her mother. I laid my head on her chest as her desperate arms clutched my little body. I could feel the lurching of her chest as it heaved with each sob. I knew she was in tremendous pain. At thirty-nine years old, already the mother of sixteen children, she was now facing a life without the love and needed personal support and company of her own beloved mother.

I quickly realized that there was nothing I could do to console her. This kind of pain ran too deep for me. I wanted to do something to help her but I felt completely helpless. Her heart was broken. She was weeping a despairing weep that I had never heard before, and I didn't want any part of that helplessness again.

I didn't ever want to have to face my life without my mother.

So if God could see things my way and just let us all die at the same moment, I thought this would be a great solution. Of course, as I got older and my siblings were getting married and having children of their own, I saw the flaw in this plan.

Now, so many years later, I was in this awful and painful position of watching my sister and her husband face the possibility of losing their child. The fear of death jumped on me again. I still had no resources to deal with coping with or accepting death. I just wanted Christy to live. I wanted us all to live, but Christy's life was of the utmost concern to my troubled mind.

Sidetracked Early On

When I had attended college in the early '70s, I had originally decided to pursue a degree in nursing, not for any valid humanitarian cause but because I thought I could make good money being a nurse. I wasn't yet attracted enough to math and science, or motivated enough, to be a medical doctor.

One sunny day, after my first semester in college, I looked up at a large hospital, and I knew that I didn't want to spend my life in one of those. I quickly changed my major to Health and Physical Education. At least I could have some fun and learn about things I loved, which were sports and the human body.

I had fun, made good grades, graduated, got a job, and then another job. I bumped around in life. I never did try to get a teaching job or concentrate on the future. I was still committed to having fun and getting by. I had some sort of fantasy that I was going to be some famous singer or actor, even though I didn't have the talent to back it up.

Now I was in my middle twenties, and the *purpose of my life* still hadn't miraculously revealed itself to me. I had lost my passion for the pursuit of psychic ability because I seemed to have no real control over when I could access the information. I lost interest in the spiritual and the mystical and got very interested in the material.

I didn't always have the conviction that *life is a journey of the soul.* I didn't know what I believed. I was now interested in having a good time, suffering as little as possible, and buying lots of stuff. I thought that this would help in my pursuit of being happy.

I was getting up in the morning, going to work, coming home, eating, watching TV, having some beer, going to bed, getting up, going to work, coming home, eating, having a martini, watching TV, going to bed, getting up, day after day, week after week, month after month, and now year after year.

Things were not changing, and neither was I—nor were the circumstances of my life. It was scary. I was not happy. I had my happy moments, but overall, I was not happy.

I think that I have always been a good person, although I haven't always acted like one. And I have, many times, done things energetically inconsistent with my personal integrity. Consequently, I have suffered a good deal more than was necessary, except that it was apparently necessary for my personal development.

I realized that my life was passing by without my figuring out what I was supposed to be doing, and I was beginning to panic. I started to look for what was wrong. I had a story book childhood complete with two wonderful parents, lots of siblings, great neighbors, and many fun times. I loved the schools I attended and the teachers who taught me. There was nothing in the past that I could point to that would help me understand why my life wasn't turning out like I thought it was supposed to.

Chapter 3

Life Is a Seminar

Seminar Junkie in the Making

In my late twenties, I started taking some seminars in personal transformation and human potential. The first thing I did was the Silva Method® course, which I loved and found very fascinating. It validated for me that I was intuitive, and it made me aware of the fact that there are techniques that help one to access their intuitive side. It also again perked my interest in natural healing. It was a course that was designed for the student to learn to focus the mind and to "tune in." At least, that's what it was to me.

I have since come to believe that the ability to control and focus the thoughts of our own minds is one of the biggest challenges of humanity. If we never learn to direct and control the thoughts that our minds think, we will not achieve true happiness. I believe this to be so because an undisciplined mind will never allow the heart to lead the way, and that is the big problem.

Shortly after doing level one of the Silva Method® I was introduced to The EST training and Werner Erhard's work (later called The Forum). It was 1980, and the radical '70s had led to radical ideas—the idea of personal transformation, the notion that we are truly responsible for the quality of our own lives and that we have everything to do with the way we "show up in life" and how life "shows up for us."

I actually liked finding out that I was responsible for the quality of my life and how I experienced my life. That notion is in the mainstream consciousness today, but in the '70s and '80s this really infuriated people.

I was not one of the furious people. I was thrilled with this ideal. It was a powerful place to be—to stand in the awareness that we are responsible for the quality of our lives. Now I was being proactive, doing something truly constructive for my life.

For years, I continued with almost everything the Forum had to offer, including participating in the assistants programs and learning to do seminar logistics. Little did I know that I was learning about energy at that time in my life.

Being on the "logistics team," I learned that setting up a seminar room "logistically correct" made a positive impact on the seminar. It was our job to make the seminar room as nondistracting as possible so that the participants could focus on the real work, the inner work. The work required total focus and complete honesty as the seminar participants reviewed their lives, relationships, communication skills, and commitments. The work also included learning to communicate the real message and to really hear others' communications. This was intense work, work which was greatly supported by a "conscious environment" in the seminar room.

Managing the "physical universe" was something I could learn. Moving chairs around and setting them in perfect rows did actually seem to make a difference in the "space" of the room, rather than having them all scattered in wiggly rows, which can be so distracting.

This was a new and thrilling concept for me—that the physical environment could make such a difference.

I continued to attend seminars during the week and on the weekends. I was a seminar junkie. I also took a six-month intensive program to learn how to lead introductory seminars. I was still unsure of what I was supposed to be when I grew up, but things were starting to come together. I was learning a lot. I think I was learning that life is a seminar!

I was moving in a much more positive direction. The fear that I was wasting my life started to subside. I still hadn't figured out what I was supposed to do with my life, but at least I was doing something I was proud of. I was sure all of this was making a difference for me.

Open and Honest? Ugh!

In these programs, I had to confront my relationship with honesty. As a child I was taught to tell the truth, and I did. I don't ever remember feeling like it was okay to lie, but somewhere in my adult life I must have started lying to myself and that seemed to seep into my relationships.

By the time I got to the EST Training, I had to confront how familiar I was with deception. That was a shocker for me. I was so unaware of how much I withheld in my communications with others, which means I wasn't being truthful. Like many in the group, I was completely unaware that withholding the truth has a similar energetic effect as lying. I had to admit to myself that I regularly withheld or twisted the truth. Yuck!

When had I fallen? When had I become this person I was meeting in this seminar?

I found myself caught up in a life full of pretense. I had been so committed to making people see a person who I thought I should be. It was a hard sell, and it took a tremendous amount of energy. It had consumed my life, and somewhere in there I had really lost myself. I had lost my sense of self worth, some of my honor and my way.

For Everything, There Is a Season...

I had to find my way back one step at a time. Fortunately, as I have experienced throughout my life, I would have helpers. It wouldn't always be the same helper. Friends would come in and out of my life like the gentle ebb and flow of the tide. Some would dance in for a short while and then out only to waltz back in five years later. Whenever I needed a friend, I always had one. God and my family were constants for me, always there whether I remembered to call on them or not. But for now, I would meet a friend for this part of the journey. This is when I met Lee.

Lee helped me to understand the things that perplexed me. She showed tremendous insight. Lee proved she could be trusted with my deepest secrets. She let me unburden my soul.

I was finally relearning the value of clean clear communications and relationships. I had a significant amount of personal healing to do. To start with this process, I had a lot of "cleaning up" to do. In pursuit of happiness I had, unintentionally, hurt or angered a lot of people, myself included.

I became very busy finding out who I was as an adult as I was cautiously peeking at my personal identity. It was a painful, important, time.

Many times I wished that I could just have avoided the decade following college and some relationships that filled it. I wished that I had exercised better judgment and would not have gone down a few of those particular roads. I now know that these times were as valuable as any other time in my life. Going through this period was my hell.

Hell, for me, was that place I mentally went when I later regretted what I did and who I did it to, and when I realized that I couldn't find a way to take it back or make it right. I found it nearly impossible to forgive myself for my own humanness.

When I started with my seminar life, this feeling began its slow but steady disappearance.

So now it was time to go on to the next phase of my relationship with seminars, with understanding the nature of health and healing and a better understanding of energy. Only this time I was going to be able to find out where God fit into this picture. It was now February of 1987, and I was about to meet my beloved teacher.

Chapter 4

Hanna Kroeger

Meeting Hanna

When I first met Hanna Kroeger, I honestly had no idea who I was about to meet and that this meeting would alter the course of my life.

I had no idea that I was going to have to learn and fully understand this energy thing to appreciate the path I had chosen to walk in this life.

It was now the seminar weekend, and Hanna would be arriving via airplane from Denver, Colorado. Lee and I went to the New Orleans Airport to scoop her up. We got there early so we could have lots of time. I wanted to make sure to impress her by doing everything right. I wanted to make a good impression so that Hanna could see that I wasn't a spiritual infant. Surely I could pull that off. After all, I am one of the seminar sponsors, aren't I? Doesn't that give me a few extra spiritual brownie points? We recognized Hanna immediately. She was the only person in the airport wearing a wool coat. It was March. We're talking New Orleans, where no one even owns a coat, and if they do, they never wear it. And if they do, they certainly never button it. With a wool coat and cap, a lovely smile, and an air of knowing, our seminar speaker had arrived. It was 1987 and Hanna was supposedly about seventy-five years old. So, if she wanted to wear her coat, fine.

We all went down the escalator to the baggage area to claim her luggage. We were totally unaware that she had merchandise and class material with her on the plane. Tom, her business manager, had already shipped us a number of boxes of books and products. However, Hanna apparently thought we needed more stuff since we were ending up with more seminar participants than we had originally thought.

Her suitcase was huge. Hanna effortlessly grabbed it off the conveyor belt and carried it along with two other bags that she had taken on board, declining all offers of help.

Well, you know how we Southerners are. We are nice. We are cordial. We are raised to be good hosts. So, when we offer a guest something, we understand that *no* means *no* only until it turns into *yes*. A good Southern host knows what her guest wants and needs more than the guest knows.

Let the Lessons Begin...

I didn't know that Hanna was a master teacher. I wasn't familiar with that concept. I thought the seminar was going to begin once we got to the church that night and the clock said 7 P.M., not at noon in the parking lot of the airport.

A lot of things I thought up until then were eventually shattered.

Walking those few steps through the parking lot, Hanna observed the exchange between Lee and me over carrying that monster bag of hers. It was obvious. We were not going to take no for an answer.

Hanna stopped walking and put the monster bag down. "What a sweet little old lady," I was thinking as we were walking. Lee and I walked a few more paces before we realized that Hanna had stopped. We turned around and walked back to her.

Ah, ha! We won! This tiny older woman had come to realize that she could, in fact, let this young, healthy, athletic thirty-two year old woman help her. I smiled. I was proud. I got my way.

I couldn't lift the bag.

I heard the groan come from deep within my own body. I felt my eyeballs enlarge and pressure build behind them. Would they pop out? This was impossible. I tried lifting the bag with two hands. I wasn't smiling anymore. I did manage to lift it off the ground. Lee had to help me carry it to the car.

Now Hanna was the one smiling.

A Master Teacher doesn't play by the rules. She doesn't wait un til the bell rings, and she hardly writes anything on the blackboard. Almost always, homework is given, but she never tells you what it is.

At least I had the good fortune to view everything that Hanna said or did as a lesson. Both Lee and Belva had told me to do that. I was glad to have that context because, otherwise, many things through the years would have made no sense at all.

Oh, No! Rev. Hanna Kroeger Is a Jesus Freak...

It only took me a few minutes into the seminar before I realized that our precious little teacher was a junkie for Jesus. This was the only thing I could see that I was going to have a problem with as far as I could tell. I would do my best to overlook this.

Prior to this seminar, I had no relationship with Jesus. To be honest, I wasn't positive He had been a real person—maybe more of a myth. The problem was that I always viewed Him as someone who would be angry with the person I had turned out to be. I had thought of Him as a finger-wagger. "You're bad, and Jesus is mad!" So, I preferred just not to think about Him.

But, throughout the seminar, Hanna would say things like, "Jesus told us to help one another. Jesus used words to heal, specific words," or, " In Jesus' name we lay the hands on this way and say the words...." And each time she would say "Jesus," I mentally changed her word to "God." That was more comfortable for me.

Before the seminar even officially started, she was working. She got out her huge wooden crucifix and placed it on the head of a very sick boy. She was away from everybody at one side of the room surrounded by his parents, commanding the demons out of him. She used a quiet but firm and powerful voice. She was not making any kind of big show, and, although I was fascinated, I was embarrassed. I had never seen anyone outside of the movie *The Exorcist* do anything like that. I did not believe in dark forces yet.

In my life there were things that I feared, but demons were not one of them. Sickness and unhappiness were what I feared the most. I had no understanding that demons or dark forces or dark energy could have any connection.

I had been afraid of disease, of sickness, and of death. I brought my knapsack of fear to that seminar. I carried it with me wherever I went, so it got into the seminar for free.

I was so fearful. I hadn't consciously realized just how fearful I was or that fear is a powerful and usually negative or debilitating *energy*.

The Seminar Begins

Her thick German accent was a challenge to us Southerners. We weren't sure if we just didn't understand her or if she just wasn't really always speaking English. She was saying things about Kantita and Foon Goos #2, apparently herbal products for Candida Albicans overgrowth. Candida? What the heck is that?

With vigilance, she pierced through the veil of ignorance determined to deliver the message she carried in her heart. Her message was that we had a duty and an obligation to learn to help ourselves and then turn around and help our fellow human beings. Her work was based on the Seven Physical Causes and the corresponding Seven Spiritual Causes of all illnesses.

The Seven Physical Causes of All Illnesses

Hanna categorized the 2,700 diseases known to modern medicine into seven categories. These seven categories made it easier for lay people to understand sickness and disease:

1. Neglect
2. Trauma
3. Congestion
4. Environmental toxins (chemical and metal poisons)
5. Worms and parasite infections
6. Infectious diseases/conditions
7. Miasms (carry over issues from our ancestors/vaccinations/and now petrochemical issues)

By making the picture of any sickness resemble that of a chain with links, the object of regaining wellness is to dismantle, one by one, any link of the chain which makes up the disease or sickness.

Hanna compared the body to the most sophisticated computer ever designed. When it is in proper working order, it can do its own work to throw off invaders and restore balance to its environment. She explained how herbs and homeopathic remedies (I had no idea what a homeopathic was) and even things like prayer could positively affect the energetic system of the human body.

Some of these theories made so much sense to me, but most of what she said made no sense at all because I wasn't even familiar with many of the terms she was using. Still, I loved every moment of it.

Prayer Directed Toward a Sick Energy Field

I did know what prayer was. I had done so much of it during peak moments of my groveling. But never had I seen prayer directed toward affecting an *energy field*, such as a disease or sickness, with the intent to change and uplift or correct the *energy* associated with that condition.

It was still sounding like a bunch of mumbo jumbo, but I liked the whole feeling of it.

It was toward the end of the seminar when I was finally seated, feeling good inside. I was confident that there was someone out there who knew something about the human body, and confident that what Hanna had told my sister to do for her daughter, Christy, would work. I was sure Christy could be helped with her mysterious disease.

As seminar host, there are many duties to attend to, so I stayed almost constantly busy throughout the seminar. By the time I got to sit down for any extended period, it was the end of the second and final day. The room was very quiet. Finally, I was able to watch Hanna and really listen to her, without being interrupted.

There was something so mesmerizing about her, and it permeated the air around her. This is what Lee must have meant about Hanna's energy field.

The whole group leaned forward in our chairs, focusing intently on her and bathing in the passion of her words as they flowed over us. We were open, our hearts delighting in her teachings, yearning to understand everything.

Hanna was speaking, and I began to be absorbed in the sounds of the silence and stillness that filled the room. It was unlike anything that I had ever experienced. She was speaking passionately, and there was such a feeling in the room, this special purity about the air. It was an *energy* that was palpable. It was as if all mind chatter in the room had stopped and there were only our hearts and souls reaching for her words.

She actually had managed to totally silence a large group of Southerners, a miracle in and of itself.

How precious was my memory of those next few moments in time! I saw her beautiful light blue aura, the energy field that surrounds and radiates from the body. I was amazed. I hadn't seen an aura before. I could see it very clearly. It surrounded Hanna so brightly and beautifully. It was the most beautiful color blue I had ever seen. I couldn't remember ever having seen that particular color blue. I later saw it in a rainbow.

I felt so happy. I was in an altered state of awareness.

"What is she saying?" I thought as I sat up on the edge of my chair and looked around. "What?"

"You have to learn to help one another. You must learn. It is you who are the Healers. Jesus said, 'Help one another.' He was talking to you. He has shown us the way; He gives us the teachings. You must learn to help yourselves. You have to learn so you can help others."

The chills were running up and down my spine from those sacred words. But what took my breath away was that there, in front of me and next to Hanna, stood Jesus. Yes, that's right. Jesus, Himself.

I have had a number of people ask me how I could be sure it was really Jesus. I had absolutely not an iota of doubt. I knew who He was instantly; I just thought I was hallucinating.

Anyway, Hanna kept calling on Jesus, and then, all of a sudden, there He was standing beside her. I was awestruck, blissed out, and, yet, confused. I was seeing and doubting and believing, all at the same time.

In the background I could still hear the passionate words of Hanna, "He healed many, and He gave us the message. 'This and more shall you do in my name.' He was talking to you. You must learn this. You must learn to help yourselves. You have to learn to help each other, alone I cannot do it."

I heard the words. I looked around to see to whom she was speaking. At first I heard "you" as meaning the person sitting next to or behind me. After about the tenth time she said it, a chord was struck in my heart, and I knew there was no place to hide. And even if I could hide from Hanna, I couldn't hide from her partner who stood beside her.

"But this is a big job, and I'm ignorant, and this is too much work, and ... I don't even know what you're talking about," I thought.

I could run away but I would only come back. But learning or even trying to learn what Hanna seemed to comprehend seemed overwhelming, incomprehensible, impossible, to me. It seemed like a lifelong task.

Somehow this seemed so unfair. I wanted someone else to have to know how to help me and my family. I wanted to go to someone else for the answers. I wanted it to be someone else's job. But it wasn't going to be. It was going to be up to me to learn. No one was coming to learn this for me, and I knew I had a responsibility to do this.

My love and understanding for Jesus began to develop instantly as I saw Him in Hanna's aura. I saw Him with my own eyes, standing next to her. He was tall and looked a little different than any of the portraits that I had seen of Him. He was serene, intense, and mesmerizing. At first, since I was questioning what it was that I was seeing I was greatly relieved when He just "evaporated." Then He came and stood on the other side of her.

She had been calling on Him. Of course He would come. Wasn't He the greatest healer of all time? Wasn't she doing the work in His name? Well, that must mean I must have been wrong all those years—He *is* real.

Since then, I have cried many times with both joy and frustration in my journey for understanding.

Hanna Sees Christy

At a break in the seminar earlier in the day, Maureen had brought Christy in to see Hanna. Hanna took one look at her, looked at the many lumps that covered her tiny body. She took out her pendulum (a device used to measure energy) and checked the energy fields. She made some hu, hu noises, looked at my sister and said in her high pitched thick German accent, "Candida and inoculation residue."

She told my sister what to do for her child. "She will be okay," Hanna assured Maureen.

Hanna didn't make much fuss over what we had perceived to be a tragedy and went on to the next thing she was doing. Just like that. We were stunned and confident at the same time. Why did we just believe her? Why were we so confident in her abilities? We didn't even know her.

The seminar continued, and then the seminar ended. Actually, it was a seminar that would continue for the rest of my life, but the actual logistical event had come to an end. And my life would never be the same. The path had taken a sudden sharp turn, and I could peek at a source of light that was previously hidden from my awareness.

Christy Heals

Clearly the things Hanna suggested for Christy were working, slowly but surely. As her body healed, other issues would seem to reveal themselves; however, each thing, as it was addressed, seemed to improve Christy's condition. There proved to be almost endless layers to this issue. Throughout this ordeal, we remembered that Hanna had taught us that dismantling a disease was like peeling an onion. Layer by layer, as you peel, what is underneath is revealed. Then that issue would be worked on.

At the point that the protozoan infection was uncovered a few years later, and the homeopathic remedies were taken, the condition finally went away for good. It has been many years now.

The fact that Hanna had been accurate with Christy and with so many others and that she was able to detect this information by accessing this invisible energy field was so fascinating to me. I had to know more.

I watched her tell numerous people what was wrong with their body or their life, just by looking at them. Time after time they would respond with surprise, "That's right. How did you know?"

Chapter 5

Ah, the Ego

The Rolex, the Pointed Gun, and the Ego

Life is a journey of the soul. So, everything we do, think, feel, and believe is a part of our soul's journey to find out what it is trying to find: lasting happiness, unconditional love, God.

The problem is, we have this little ego. Usually we consider ourselves to be whatever it is our ego identifies with, and this leads us to all kinds of side roads.

But what is the ego? And what does that mean, "whatever the ego identifies itself with"?

I started to get the distinction between my self, the real Self, and my ego with a particularly upsetting occurrence. It was the early '80s. My friend Johnny and I had gone out to a party and then to a bar. Once we got to the bar, we decided that a quiet backgammon game was more inviting than that crowded smoky bar, so we left to go to my home.

When we were getting back in the car after leaving the bar, we were robbed at gunpoint. I had many items in my car, including a brand new designer purse, a brief case full of store deposits for the store that I was managing, and an assortment of jewelry. My gold Rolex watch was on my wrist.

The doors to the car were pulled open so fast that neither of us ever saw the two men before their arms were in our car. The guy with the gun demanded that Johnny get out of the car as he reached into the car and grabbed the keys from the ignition. I was still in the passenger's seat. I thought that I was going for a ride. I thought I was facing rape, and, quite frankly, rape was quickly starting to seem like an okay idea. I would cooperate. I just wanted to live.

The angry demanding face without the gun was screaming at me to give him my jewelry. As I was taking off my rings, new gold necklace, and bracelet, I could hear Johnny arguing with the gunman. "Shut up, Johnny," I remember thinking. "Shut up or they are going to kill us both."

That was the last time I remember thinking of Johnny during this episode. Now the robber was demanding my watch, and my ego snapped in and took over.

"I don't have one!" I heard my defiant ego say.

I knew he had not seen my beauty, as it was hidden underneath my jacket sleeve. I had paid $1,300 (second hand), I had financed it and sacrificed to have that babe, and I wasn't givin' it to anybody! There was more shouting and words from the three males, but my robber had bought my quick lie and did not pursue the demand for my watch.

Everything was happening so quickly. I was soon to get my turn with the gunman. Now the one with the gun was in my face. The robbers had traded places after opening the trunk, grabbing my leather briefcase and whatever else was there. They already had most of our valuables, my purse, money, credit cards, jewelry, Johnny's wallet, and his honor. Now the gun was in my face, and my tight jeans insisted that the gunman cop a feel while I looked down the barrel.

See, the ego's job is to look good. In this case, looking good definitely meant having a gold Rolex watch. The ego was prepared to win this battle. Apparently, who I considered myself to be, my personal identity, was not with my Higher Self, my body, my honor, or my life, but with my gold Rolex watch. My ego was in control of the situation, and it totally identified itself with that damn watch. It needed that watch.

Who I was at that moment was not Ginger, child of God, lover of life. Who I was, was my watch. Apparently I was willing to die for this false identification.

When the gunman struck me across that face with the back of his hand, I was relieved. Somehow I knew that this meant they were leaving, and they did. They gave Johnny back the car keys, and we chased them down the street. We were all moving in the same direction, we by car and they on foot. They were carrying my beautiful leather briefcase stuffed with many symbols of my false identifications, things that I thought at the time measured my self-worth.

Later, Johnny and I spent many sorrowful moments as we each gingerly admitted to the other that when our survival was at stake, neither of us remembered to think of the other. I had an even harder time admitting that it was because I was too busy thinking of my precious gold Rolex watch.

If I Am Not Who My Ego Considers Me to Be, Then Who Am I?

Who are we, if not the ego, the personality, or the body? We have an ego. We need it. It has a job to do. Its job is to help us survive. We have a personality. It gives expression to the self. We have a body which is the vehicle of the soul for expression in this incarnation, in this life. But we are not just our personality nor our body nor our soul.

Who we really are is an expression of the love of God. We are a part of the One Spirit. We each have varying amounts of love in our hearts and that is what defines who we are.

In this journey as a human, we forget that we are one with the spirit of God. This identification with things other than the one spirit of God, this sense of being separated from God, causes us great confusion and great pain. It causes us the pain of human existence instead of the experience of the joy of God's blissful creation.

On this life's journey, the love that we are wants to know that it is connected with God, the Creator. The real self pursues the inner state, the inner world, the kingdom of God within. It may have to search down many dead end paths and trails in search of something it doesn't even consciously know it's in search of. But somewhere deep inside, it is searching for the only thing that will fill that void and that sense of longing, and that is God and the experience of love and oneness.

The real self doesn't care about getting credit for accomplishments

33

or good deeds. The real self wants to be an expression of the love of God. The real self wants to live in harmony with the will of God. The ego does not feel that God is the missing ingredient or that there is anything that God can do or give us that it can't.

The ego thinks it is not so cool to seek God. Most egos want power, money, fame, but all egos want control, absolute and unquestionable control over your life and over the way others think of you. The ego's job is to survive and to control. Anything that the ego considers itself to be is what it will attempt to control and protect, such as a job, a reputation, a title, status in society, a new car, a relationship, control over others' religious beliefs, or even a watch.

My ego protected my gold Rolex watch. I still have that watch. It doesn't work. It hasn't in years. I've tried to have it fixed, but there's something wrong with it that it doesn't keep time. It was never for keeping time anyway. It was for looking good. It still does that. It looks good in my drawer. I keep it as a reminder. I almost traded my life for it.

I want to clarify a point. There is nothing inherently wrong with owning a gold Rolex watch or any other possession. My watch was beautiful, and I truly enjoyed wearing it. It's just that later, I was horrified at having risked my life for it. I was clear that it was a totally egotistical thing to do, and although I could recognize the difference between myself and my ego, one little gun incident was not going to keep my ego quiet and in its rightful place. Oh, no. This battle with the ego was going to be a lifelong task, I was to find out.

I had a few glimpses of my ego being under my command instead of my being under its control, but those glimpses were few and far between. I was having moments of being in touch with the real self that yearns to experience God in the eyes of a friend, in the laugh of a companion, in the feel of the wind and the beauty of a flower, or the face of a loved one.

The ego thinks there's too much fuss being made over this happiness fantasy. The ego wants power and control and doesn't want to have to fight God for it.

Meeting Hanna was not good news for my ego. She managed to beat it up and send it packing many times. She didn't seem to mind going to battle with it because she knew she would always win. Still, it must have been a nuisance for her. It showed up all the time.

Although my ego had always been in total control of my life, my spirit and soul yearned for the likes of Hanna. Meeting Hanna was meeting someone who had a direct relationship with God, not one she only read about in a book. She was someone whose soul had been on this journey and with whom God seemed to be well pleased.

How did I know this? Well, it seemed she could work miracles, that she could heal the sick and make lovers of God out of the most estranged of us. She did this with such assurance, and she never "preached" at us. She knew God. That was clear. He knew her. That, too, was clear. It was a personal relationship. It seemed to permeate the air around her. It wasn't in the words she said, it was in her everything.

She was the Godliest person I had ever met. She had a faith I had never encountered. She had an understanding that seemed to surpass anyone else's. I thought she was a saint and a smart one. I didn't understand much of anything that she had been teaching us, but I knew I wanted some of what she had. Besides that, she was just fascinating. She picked up on everything.

I remember my younger brother standing up at that first seminar to ask Hanna a question about his backache. She said, "Well, your kidneys don't work properly."

"That's right," he said in amazement. "How do you know that?"

"Well, I can look at you and tell," she said matter-of-factly.

Over and over again, whether the problem was physical, emotional, or mental, she could tell. Usually just by looking at the person.

One time my sister Kathy went to Boulder for the summer retreat with me. I hadn't told Hanna anything about my sister, but I had always thought that this particular sibling was extra special. Half way through the class and on a break, I thought I would ask Hanna what she thought.

"She has very pure thoughts," Hanna said lovingly.

It was true. Kathy is the sweetest and most genuinely good person that I know besides my own mother. Her thoughts indeed were good. Kathy is several years older than I, and I had never seen her be unkind to or about anything or anyone. How did Hanna know that just by looking at her in class?

What was it that she was seeing? Was it auras? Auras are fascinating.

"I want to see what she sees. I want to see auras and other things," I thought. "I just want to be able to see what she is seeing."

Make sure you are ready to get what you ask for. If you want "to see," fine, but it's not all pretty, as I was soon to find out.

Chapter 6
Forces of Darkness and Light

I remember a few of my startling brushes with coming to the awareness that dark forces really do exist. The dark forces or negative entities are energies that are "lower vibrations."

Lower vibration? No vibration. What did that mean? I had heard Hanna use terms like those many times, and I really didn't know what they meant exactly. I had quickly understood that it wasn't good when things had no or low vibration. I had also realized that it was good and healthy when things had high vibration. The high vibration beings and things were light or of the light. The things with no or low vibrations were not of the light, were not harmonious, and didn't help us.

I had heard Hanna say that angels had a very high vibration. Someone else said that angels were so high in vibration that if they wanted to appear to humans in our denser third dimensional reality, that they would have to slow down or lower their vibration so that we would be able to perceive them with our eyes. It seems we ordinarily have limitations which allow us to perceive only a denser dimension of reality.

I had heard Hanna talk about demons and dark forces as having low or no vibration. I could conceptualize this, but I didn't understand that this was energy.

I guess at this time, I just started mentally to categorize things as "above this invisible line" where things were higher in vibration and "below the line" where things were denser, darker, and not as harmonious. I did not realize that this subconscious categorization would later lead me to a very easy way to understand energy.

Demons in Texas

It was 1987, the summer after first meeting Hanna. Lee and I had already gone to Hanna's Retreat in Boulder, Colorado, but we wanted to go again. We just wanted to be around Hanna and her teachings. We felt that we actually needed the tremendous nurturing that being in her energy field was sure to provide again. We didn't want to have to wait another year.

Lee, my sister Dottie, and I packed up Lee's car and headed to the mountains. We were driving from New Orleans, Louisiana, to Boulder, Colorado, a 1,500-mile trip, so we would have to drive two or three days to get there.

Around midnight of the first night we were in a small town in Texas, and we got one of our first lessons in *lower vibration energies*.

We stopped to get a motel room. We were all so exhausted and sleepy, and though we had wanted to get farther down the road, a terrible storm kicked up right as we entered town. From the silence and stillness of a dark Texas night, we were suddenly captivated by the wind and rain and by the fact that our radar detector went off again and again. This should have been our first clue because each tenth of a mile it would beep again. But it was raining so hard we could not see to continue driving and resigned ourselves to stopping at this little radar buzzing motel.

Lee and I wanted to check out the room before we committed to take it.

I still can't exactly describe what happened then or how we experienced the room, but something was very wrong. We practically threw the key back to the desk clerk behind the glass barricade. We definitely ran back to the car to find an equally terrorized Dottie, wide eyed and shaking, in the back seat of the car.

We peeled out of that parking lot and flew out of town, shrieking. Having rolled down all the windows in the car, we were all yelling at the top of our voices, demanding that these energies leave us alone. We would look at each other and see other beings looking back at us, and we'd scream all the louder. It was an ugly sight.

When we got out of the city limits, the storm stopped. When we finally felt that they had released us and that we were somewhat safe, we tried to explain to each other what we thought had happened.

Dottie said that while we were checking out the motel room she started having the most foreboding feeling. For the first time, ever, she felt in fear of losing her life.

I said that the room was nice enough, it seemed clean, but when Lee looked down at something on the night stand and turned her head to me, she didn't look like Lee anymore, and she said I didn't look like Ginger. We both felt like someone had been or was going to be murdered in that room or that something equally vile was going to happen, and we didn't want it to be us. Something, some energy, was still there, and it was horrible. We were so freaked out.

Now these energies had somehow attached themselves to us, perhaps looking for a piggyback ride. We were rookies in the work and did not know how to release them. We apparently had allowed the attachment through our fear and our doubt. If we had walked into the motel room with strength and confidence (and perhaps full of a lot more love than we were radiating at that time), then nothing could have touched us. Our force field, or energy field, would have been so strong we could have walked into this hell without being affected and definitely without these energies attaching to us. But that is not what happened. We were terrified and terrorized, and we had a weakness in our field that would allow these lower, denser, darker energies to attach to us.

We hadn't yet learned what to do except to holler at them in the name of Jesus, commanding them to leave, which they have to do when you do that. So that's what we did, over and over again, until we were hoarse.

At least now all of our sleepiness was gone, and we were awake, totally awake, and able to drive for a few more hours.

I remember thinking: Is this what we have to go through to get there? Is it true, is there something or someone or some beings that really do have the ability to put obstacles in our path to keep us from seeking the company of one of God's people?

I just wanted to see Hanna, now more than ever. But I did not want my lessons and this journey for understanding to have to be so confronting. Perhaps this was just a onetime fluke.

I was going to Boulder to learn about herbs and healing. I thought healing was about the physical body and things you can see. I had heard Hanna talk about entities and negative energies, but I never even watch scary movies. So, I had no intention, nor had I yet seen, any need of going deeper into the subject.

We finally got to a safe hotel room in a well-lighted city, our lessons being ended for the night.

Eventually we got to Colorado.

Hanna was not surprised about our little ghost story and in her usual style, paid little attention to our drama and recounting of the details. However, she was quite familiar with the town we encountered and casually offered, "That place has no vibration."

I didn't exactly know what that meant, but I knew that we would take a different route home.

Of course, the summer retreat was wonderful. We had arrived in Boulder on Thursday afternoon. The session started that night and lasted through the weekend. Hanna had a large and very simple retreat center (which was also her home) in the valley. Everything was quiet and peaceful. As we drove down the gravel road, and her house came into view, I had the warmest and safest feeling in my heart.

I felt a little foolish as I remembered the first time I had seen Hanna's property only a few months prior. I had looked at the land, at the plants, the grass, and the weeds with no appreciation or understanding of nature. I was looking through different eyes and had the thought that, as a gift, sometime in the future, I would like to hire a landscape architect for Hanna. That way they would tidy the place and get rid of all of these miscellaneous weeds and plants and put in some nice beds and shrubs and planters.

On the classes herbal walk on Saturday, not only could Hanna name every miscellaneous plant and "weed" but she could also list its healing or medicinal properties.

"Wow," I remembered thinking, "I am really an out of touch, ignorant, materialistic snob."

So now, as I was seeing this same land for a second time, I was grateful for my new perspective. Hanna showed so much respect for the land, for the flowers, the trees and all of nature, including the insects. Hanna knew that consciousness exists in all things, not just in people. It took me years to truly get that one. But Hanna never said to us, " Hey you should respect the land, you should love Mother Earth, you should talk to the flowers and the nature spirits and respect the grass and the mud and the rocks that you walk on." She never made that speech; she just was so honoring and respecting of nature that it eventually touched our awareness and our hearts.

Anyway, the summer retreat school was great, again. We learned how fantastic and resilient the human body is and how it is always seeking balance. We found out that you can use herbs, homeopathics, vitamins, minerals, and hands-on techniques to help the body balance itself. We had a fresh dose of inspiration. Now it was Monday morning, time to go.

Let's Confront That Fear of Flying

I was driving back with Lee, Dottie, and Lee's daughter, Chrissy, who had met us in Colorado. I was only going to be with them until Dallas, where I was to board an airplane in order to make it to New Orleans in time for a business meeting.

I was still intensely afraid of flying. I avoided it whenever possible. I was afraid of dying. Some of my well-meaning friends had told me that I was really afraid of not being in control. No matter what anyone said, it never lessened the fear.

So I decided to seek some advice from Hanna. Actually I asked her if she thought I was going to make it to New Orleans alive. I was looking for a little sympathy or a little encouragement. I knew she was so intuitive that if I were going to die, she would be able to forewarn me or tell me not to get on that plane. Then I would blow off the business meeting, finish the drive back with Lee, Dot, and Chrissy, and live happily ever after.

Hanna looked at my pitiful state, and instead of coddling me she gave me a sharp look. With a very serious tone laced with a hint of laughter, she came at me saying, "You better make it! You are responsible for everyone on that plane. You'd better make sure they make it!"

"What?" I said in utter disbelief.

Now, I had done all those seminars in human potential and personal transformation. It was true that I had come to the realization that I was, in fact, responsible for the quality of my life; but the thought that I was, in any way, responsible for a plane full of strangers was just a little too far out of my reach.

"You are responsible for everyone on that airplane. You better make sure they make it."

41

She did say what I thought she said. She said it again.

"When you get on that plane, check and make sure the girls in the uniforms have vibration. Make sure all the people have vibration. The aura does not want to be involved in a disaster and will leave the body prior to such an accident. So check everybody out."

"Then," Hanna continued, "start praying. Pray for the pilot and the copilot and the crew. Ask that God would protect them throughout the flight. Then pray for each and every person on that plane, and see the light of Christ shinning through them and protecting them. After you finish with them, pray for the mechanics, the luggage guys, then the air traffic controllers. Don't miss anyone."

Then she said, "Also, ask God for seven of his angels to protect the plane. See them as seven different colored angels. Put a yellow one, or whatever color you choose, at the nose of the plane and a red one at the tail. Position the angels around the plane, and talk to them. Pray to them. Prayer is the vibration that allows the angels to fly."

I guess Hanna didn't stop to consider that I might never have seen an angel or the fact that I wasn't totally sure they really existed. I guess Hanna didn't check to see if my limited concepts or beliefs actually concurred with her instructions. There she was, doing it again, interacting with me as though I actually had faith and understanding.

An Airport Angel

When I was dropped off in the predawn hours at the Dallas-Fort Worth Airport, I was stir crazy from having driven all night. I was dropped off at a place where I would have to take a shuttle to the proper air terminal. This airport is ridiculously large, and I was unfamiliar with shuttle systems.

I found myself staring up at all these color-coded terminal markings, trying to figure out which shuttle to get on and where I would need to get off, when it suddenly dawned on me that not one thing on the board made any sense to me. I was reading words but they were not registering anywhere in my brain. I started to panic. There was no one around. It was only me, and I had lost my ability to read or use my brain right there in the Texas airport.

I kept looking around, out the door, at the shuttles coming and going, and then back at the instruction board. Nothing was happening. I started to cry, feeling totally helpless and frustrated.

All of a sudden, there was a man standing next to me. I did not see or hear him walk in the door, and I was standing gazing at the door and the instruction board.

"Where are you going?" he asked me, as if he had been standing there a while observing my despair.

I told him the name of the airline. He looked at the board and told me what I needed to do. When the shuttle arrived and the door opened, he told me to get in and then boarded this shuttle with me. I was so relieved.

"Where have you been?" he asked.

While trying to look composed and attempting to find the words that could explain Hanna and what she did and what I was learning, I noticed that this attractive man had no luggage and no apparent destination. He never spoke about himself, and when my stop came, he told me that it was time to get off. He also made sure I knew in which direction to walk. He did not get off with me.

I was still so delirious. I got off the shuttle and immediately said, "Thank you, God. He was an angel." I heard myself. I heard my own words. Then I thought, "Naaa, it couldn't be. Angels don't wear blue jeans."

Through the years, I have thought of him many times.

When I got on the plane I quickly pulled out my pendulum, hiding it from view. I pointed my left hand at a few passengers. When the pendulum gave a strong positive swing on four or five people, I decided that it was safe to assume that the people had auras, and I started to get to my other work.

By the time I finished praying for everybody Hanna had told me to pray for, the flight was almost over. I didn't have time to be nervous. I had too much work to do.

I fly a lot now. It doesn't bother me. I go through my same ritual as instructed by Hanna, although a shortcut version, and I usually even affectionately name the plane and talk to it.

I marvel in the brilliance of Hanna's teaching. She gave me something so useful and constructive to occupy my mind, a mind that would otherwise have been used to put a lot of fear energy into the trip. Instead of my mind participating in the "below the line" activity of worry and fear, it was focused toward supporting the work of the heart. It was, therefore, able to vibrate with the loving energy of prayer and good will.

It was a reminder to me that we are spiritual beings and we are always in God's hands, every moment, every hour of everyday. Whether we realize that we are a part of the One Spirit in all, whether we think we deserve the love of God and the protection of the angelic beings or not, we are a part of God who loves us and, with His angels, protects us. We are spiritual beings with physical bodies. We are always loved and always connected to God and the higher realms.

Chapter 7

Intuition

Reading with the Third Eye

In the spring of 1988, I had just finished writing a book, and I was going to try to get it published. First I wanted to make sure that it was good, not just good reading, but also honest and accurate.

We were on our way to a seminar with Hanna sitting in the back seat of the car. I was in the front seat, and I reached back and handed Hanna a copy of the final draft. She didn't open it, didn't ask me any questions, she just held it. Then, as if she was trying to swat a fly on her forehead, she smacked the book to her third-eye center, held it there a few seconds, and then said, "It is a good book, a children's book, it is the truth, it will help children." My jaw dropped, as did my friend's. How did she know it was a children's book? How could she look through the binder with her forehead?

I never quite got used to all she could do. I never got to the place where she ceased to amaze me. It must have taken her years to learn to   direct and focus the thoughts of her mind so well that she could read through a plastic binder with her third eye. Who is this woman? What is it she has? How did she get it? How can I get some of it, too? I want to be just like her.

For years, after our initial meeting, I wanted to be Hanna, until I got a glimpse of what it really meant to be Hanna.

Want to Be Good with Energy? Start by Telling the Truth, the Whole Truth, Nothing But the Truth

I wanted to make a difference. I wanted to do good things. I wanted to help people, and I wanted to feel good about my life. I was willing to work hard and do what it took, as long as I didn't have to suffer.

There were things I was finding out about this journey; it wasn't necessarily going to be easy. And it would require honesty. Complete and total honesty. Ugh.

Later, I came to understand that if we don't get to that place of complete honesty, we never learn to be great with energy and reading energy fields. That isn't to say that we have to go broadcasting our life or the secrets of our soul, but we must be able to tell the truth to ourselves about ourselves. There can be nothing hidden.

And to be good with energy we must be trustworthy. This is what worked for me about my friendship with Lee. She was trustworthy. If I told her something in confidence, it remained confidential.

I had a good foundation now, with understanding the general rules of communication from Werner Erhard's teachings. They went something like this: *What is the thing that needs to be said between you and another so that love is all that is there? What is that communication that needs to happen so that you can get on with the business of loving each other? What is that thing that you are unwilling to communicate, the communicating of which could totally clear up a situation and allow you to have a real relationship?*

Many of us live as though we can get away with not having to be that clean in our communications. We think we can hide or conceal things. But, energetically, the cost is much too great, and "that thing" that we need to say or express doesn't really go away; it waits for another time.

In my quest for understanding and applying the principles of energy, I had to answer some difficult questions: *Are you telling yourself the truth about who and what you are? Are you honest about yourself to others? Do you paint an acceptable picture of yourself for others? Do they like you better because you show a picture of who you think they want you to be? Do you like you better?*

I had to ask myself: *At what price is your soul for sale? At what price does your self respect go? For what will you offer up your personal integrity? Why would you sell out the power that your honesty has for you?*

Why do we sideswipe ourselves energetically by working so hard to put up and keep up a false front?

Let's See If I Can Hide from Hanna and See If She Can Still Find Me

One day, after a few years of being around Hanna, I called her because I was feeling sick. I felt awful. Hanna was so intuitive she could tell me over the phone what was wrong and what to do. I was at Lee's house. We were doing some good work, and I felt secure that Hanna would pick up from the energy coming over the phone that we were following her instructions and helping others. If she didn't pick up on it, that would be okay, because I would be sure to work it into the conversation.

Anyway, I was in Lee's sweet little home office when I made the call. Hanna took a while before she gave me her answer. Her tone was short and direct, almost scolding.

"You poisoned yourself," she said.

"Oh," I wiggled around. "Yes, we may have too much incense burning in this room." (Maybe she'd go for that one).

"No," she said sternly, "you poisoned yourself." And she hung up the phone.

"Damn, she is good. Ugh, I feel naked."

I was so ashamed. I had done it, and now she knew it too. I had a hangover. I wished I could take that call back. I wished she didn't know. But, on some level, I was glad she knew. On some level, it was a relief. I hadn't yet had the courage to tell myself that I was hiding my relationship with alcohol, but now someone else knew. Someone I couldn't lie to. She wasn't going to insist that I make promises that I wasn't ready to keep, she couldn't make me. I was the only one who could, but now I knew that she knew. She knew that I knew that she knew.

I never tried to hide anything from her again. What use would it be? This little incident happened in 1988. After this time, I started to get more serious about my own healing and the healing work I needed to learn and understand.

Chapter 8
Working with Energy Fields

Shortly after our first seminar with Hanna, Lee and I had decided that we needed to have her products available in New Orleans in case our family and friends got sick or needed help.

We each got a bookshelf, and little by little we filled them with herbal remedies, books, and homeopathics.

A year or so later, we decided to get a group together once a week at my house to practice and share Hanna's teachings, so that we could learn it better.

Still completely enamored with Hanna and the work, I was attempting to live a double life. I thought that I could be an Herb Queen during the week and a party-holic on the weekends. I thought the two ways would balance each other out. They don't, but it is a good place to start. Eventually one would have to go, but I would have to find this out the hard way.

With two others, I rented an apartment in an old Victorian house in uptown New Orleans. The rooms were quite large, and it was a good gathering place.

Clearing Negative Energy

We would start each class by doing a seven candle ceremony that Hanna had taught us, to clear all of us of any possible entities or negative energies. One night we were doing this procedure, and we could not get the negative energies to release. When you can't get a release, you know it. A "release" is when the lower, denser vibration (or dark force) actually leaves or transmutes (and hopefully goes to the light).

The hair was still prickly on my arms, and I had kind of a creepy feeling. We worked and worked at it, and I tried saying the words more firmly. "In the name of Jesus get out of here, get out of here." Nope. No release.

This was the one and only time I was ever able to reach Hanna by phone at night. I called. She answered.

"Hanna, this is Ginger. We have a group over at my house. We are doing the seven candle ceremony, and we can't get a complete release."

"Hold the phone up in the air so I can see what is there," Hanna said to me. Of course, this didn't even seem like an odd request to me anymore. So, I did it.

"Oooohhhh," she said, "you got a big one there!"

Okay, don't panic. Stay calm. I was talking to myself. I knew better then to let myself become afraid, but I was teetering somewhere near that edge.

"What can we do?" I sheepishly asked Hanna.

"Have everybody go over to the window. Open the window, and everyone point out the window and yell, 'Rockma!'"

"What does that mean?" I asked sheepishly.

"It doesn't matter," she commanded. "The dark forces don't like that vibration."

Then, she hung up the phone.

We went to the window and followed Hanna's instruction. Immediately we felt that presence leave. It was a tough depossession, and I had judgmental thoughts about the creepy guy who brought the possession in my home. At the time, I believed that if a person had a possession, it absolutely meant that they were a bad person. I didn't want that guy in my house again or in my life. But at least we had another way to get a release if any of those evil people did come back around.

Objects Can Hold a Negative Energy

On another occasion, we did some work on a skeletal chart. Hanna had shown us that you can check the energy of a person's skeletal system, find out where the energy is not flowing right, and–with the power of the spoken word–ask in the name of Jesus for that bone or vertebra to go back to its rightful place. She said that God knew where that bone was supposed to be, and the bone knew where it was supposed to be so it didn't matter that we didn't know because it wasn't us who was really doing the healing anyway.

She showed us that you could take a pencil or a small wooden peg and a small mallet and tap on the pencil or peg in the area that the bones needed alignment, while focusing the mind and prayer to the skeletal structure. Then she would tap, tap, tap and say, "See? Healed!"

Well, I didn't really see anything happening, but sometimes the person she was working on would say they could feel it, so I considered it was possible, but just a bit too goofy to be real. The skeletal chart work was a fascinating concept, but I really didn't believe in it. Although I did accept that in God's world all things are possible, still I thought it was highly unlikely that God would need us to bang on a skeletal chart to heal someone's bones. Regardless, I showed others what Hanna had shown me, and they seemed to think there was possibly something to it.

Hanna had told us to use a laminated skeletal chart and the person's picture or saliva sample. She definitely said laminated. I heard it like we had some sort of option not to use laminated. Since I didn't really believe in that particular work anyway, what difference would it make?

So, instead of telling anyone that I did not really believe this, I decided to see if anything would happen. I did quite a few different people (using their saliva sample) on a nice, big non-laminated paper skeletal chart that hung on the wall of my home office. After I would finish using it I would go hang it back up in my office. I had not considered that the lamination would keep the persons energy from absorbing into the paper.

One day, I went into the office and nearly jumped out of it in one leap. I swear I saw the skeletal chart looking back at me. I instantly realized it was possessed. I called in my two roommates to see if they could see it. I figured, if they saw it, then it really was not my imagination. They were not much into the work, but they were both open-minded people.

They were so freaked out when they saw it. There was no doubt to them and, consequently, no doubt to me. There was some entity or dark force or energy looking back at us that had not been there before. Confirmation, once again, to always follow Hanna's instructions. But for now, I had to go burn that skeletal chart.

We Are Bound at the Level of Our Own Judgments

Hanna came back to town to do another seminar the next year and then again the next. I was still being a party-holic on the weekends and Herb Queen during the week. This had gone on for some time now, but I was taking my herbs and learning about energy and spiritual stuff, so I felt safe enough.

My life was starting to get a little bumpy again, the glow of a new relationship having worn off and the reality of life setting in. I was working and drinking too much, and this made me lazy, cranky, and out of balance. I found comfort in Hanna's work, although I had little time for it.

It was time for Hanna to come to town again. I loved hosting her seminars, and also I felt really important. From the heart side of my being, I was completely honored for the chance to be in Hanna's presence again and to help make this available for others too. The work was clearly making a difference in many of our lives.

From the ego side of my being, I was overly proud and cocky about my role. It seemed that I was completely committed to the seminar participants believing that I had attained some level of health and spirituality that they had not. This was not a conscious thought, but it was apparently a driving force.

I was only fooling myself, of course.

Looking back, I can see where the ego was leading me.

I have seen many of us allow our egos to do ridiculous and even cruel things in the name of spirituality.

What Causes the Energy Field to Be Out of Balance?

I was trying to help myself and others by hosting Hanna's seminars. I was striving to be a better person and to be closer in my relationship to God.

Each time Hanna would come do a seminar, some miracle would happen. Also, after each seminar, I would realize that I understood the material better or that things that I had not previously understood now made sense. The pieces were fitting together better both on a physical and a spiritual level.

I had already learned an amazing amount of information about the way the body worked and about the nature of different diseases and conditions. I understood certain diseases that, prior to Hanna, I had not even heard of. Hanna would tell us not to get caught up in the names of diseases because not all diseases (by the same name) are caused by the same thing.

For example, one person's arthritis might be caused by a staph infection while another's is caused by a parasitic infection, yet another's might be from a dog virus. Often it is more than one condition coming together to create a disease.

"How is it manifesting in the body?" she would question. This would give the clue as to where to go and look for the answer.

Each person was different, and she wanted us to keep our minds open.

For example, the reason one woman could not get pregnant might be because her partner had the mumps virus (from not having a good case of the mumps or from having a mumps inoculation); whereas, another woman's reason for not getting pregnant might be that she had measles residue in her ovaries or some other cyst-causing organism in there. (Again, possibly from not having a good case, not resting when she did have them, or from being vaccinated with the virus).

One of my sisters kept miscarrying after already having three children. Hanna checked her out and said, "Lung flukes."

"Lung flukes?" I questioned.

"Lung flukes," Hanna said again. She had checked the energy output of Lily's bronchi, and it was low. She had said the name of a remedy (words are energy), and then she checked again, and the bronchi showed a high vibration.

"The baby can't get enough oxygen because the mother has lung flukes."

Honestly, I thought this was one of those times that Hanna was going to be off her mark, but a few months and a seven dollar bottle of lung flukes homeopathic later, Lily was pregnant with my niece Caitlin.

But as much as I was learning the technical or "scientific" side of health and healing, I was learning that Hanna's heart was always engaged in the process. This was the major key. Without it the rest of the work is lost.

Chapter 9

Hanna Helps Me

Hanna's Background

Hanna was brilliant besides being intuitive. She was the daughter of missionaries and was consequently raised with the awareness of needing to help others. She had also been a nurse in a natural healing hospital in Dresden, Germany, and had worked with the best doctors there. Germany has a long history in using what we call "natural healing methods" and "natural remedies," so she had gotten quite an education.

She earned an N.D. (Naturopathic Doctor) degree while in Germany. Although she had her N.D. from Germany, she quickly learned that it meant nothing but trouble here in the United States because, until recently, no one even knew what it was. And since it wasn't an M.D., her degree wasn't taken seriously.

That didn't keep her from knowing what she knew, and throughout her life, she continued to educate herself on a daily basis. Over the years she acquired as students many medical doctors, as well as other scientists, as each realized that she seemed to have a better grasp of healing than anyone else.

I think Hanna was always a little miffed at the fact that she believed that the American Medical Association (A.M.A.) thought it had all the answers for healing or that they were in complete control over who can heal. She thought it was a ridiculous notion that only people with licenses could be good at healing. Jesus didn't have a license to heal and He didn't go to medical school. She didn't think that the A.M.A., the drug industry, or even the scientists had as good an understanding or talent for healing as mothers naturally do.

Mothers, Women, and Healers

Hanna thought mothers and women in general were the most natural healers because it is the basic nature of woman to nurture. She considered that healing was a total person phenomenon, not just a physical body thing, and that a mother's songs could heal and a mother's touch could heal. She felt that women were more naturally intuitive, and a mother would go to the ends of the earth to figure out how to heal her child or family member if she had to.

Nevertheless, this belief didn't stop Hanna from working with many men who were interested in healing and who became her students. Some of them became excellent teachers and healers. It was just that she would almost become indignant if a woman didn't show interest in doing what Hanna perceived was her obligation to do (which was learning to take care of herself and her family by learning about health and healing). She felt that we should do it as naturally as possible and that most of the work should be done in the home.

Hanna was driven by the desire to learn as much as she could so she could help her youngest daughter, Lisa. Lisa had never recovered from the polio vaccination, and she is what we now understand to be autistic. I will tell you that story a little later on.

My Little Problem

So here it was again time for Hanna to come to town to do another seminar. My enthusiasm was in full bloom for this event, as always, but this time I also had a personal need I was confident Hanna could help me with. I was having a pesky little physical problem that just would not clear up no matter what I tried. With Hanna coming for a seminar, I knew it would be easy for her to detect and easy for me to clear up once Hanna gave me the remedy.

During these seminars Hanna would check everyone out with her pendulum to see what it was that they needed. She was checking energy fields to see if the person's energy field resonated with the frequency of the herbs and the homeopathic remedies.

She would do this checking in three separate groups as she finished discussing the issues for that section. For example, on the first night she would check for the remedies for congestion. The next morning she would check for chemical and metal toxin issues, as well as for worms and parasites.

Again, she would do this by checking the energy fields of the body and seeing what products would help to bring that energy field up to a healthier, higher vibration.

Usually a person would show that they would benefit from taking numerous things because, let's face it, most of us are in less-than-optimum health.

I was quite proud since the first go 'round showed that I didn't need anything.

I was quite proud when, on the second set of issues, I still didn't show the need for anything.

Each time, I made sure that enough of the seminar participants saw that I was healthy and, therefore, better and more progressed than they. (My ego was in heaven.) I was the only one not showing the need for anything. I was proud, proud.

On the third and final set, Hanna checked me and again said, "Nothing. You don't need anything."

Now I was worried. I had been bleeding vaginally for a couple of months, and it wasn't my period. It was stinky, too, as was the rest of my body, although I was bathing three times a day. Now this time I didn't want the seminar participants to know my business, so I whispered to Hanna, "But Hanna, I am bleeding vaginally, it is not my period, and I stink. Every orifice of my body stinks, and I am bathing constantly."

The "Possession"

Hanna stepped back from me and looked deep into my eyes. She pulled a little cube out of her pocket that was filled with some powdery herbs and told me to hold my left hand out. She placed that odd little cube in my outstretched hand, and her pendulum flew around so fast it looked like a helicopter.

Following my lead to let the seminar participants know how I was doing, she shouted at the top of her voice in her thick, but distinct German accent, "Oh, honey, you have a demonic possession!"

I gasped, as did the rest of the group. Across the sea of eyes glaring at me in horror were those of my dear mother.

If I could have crawled under the carpet, I surely would have. I knew right away that she was right, and it made all the smells and the angry fits make sense.

"What can we do?" I asked her desperately.

"Send me a photograph," Hanna said flatly.

I knew that she did most of her spiritual depossession work with photos, but I didn't have a photo of myself with me, I just had me and this thing.

"But, Hanna," I whimpered, "you can't leave me like this! Now that I know what it is, I can't stand myself."

"Okay," she relented. "Give me your saliva sample. I will do the work from that when I get back home."

It was like the parting of the Red Sea when I walked away from Hanna and through the crowd of seminar participants. I felt like a leper.

Finally it was time to take Hanna to the airport for her trip back home to Boulder. Hanna always insisted on being able to leave late Saturday afternoon so that she could make it back to lead her church service on Sunday morning.

I was grateful that I would have some time alone for Lee and Hanna to console and comfort me.

That did not happen.

Neither Lee nor Hanna would even look at me.

Lightning Strikes

That night, it was time to go to bed. I was staying at a friend's house. There were three other people in the house. I don't know why I thought that Hanna was going to get me released from this awful possession that night, but I did.

When it was time to go to bed, I drank one beer to be relaxed. That's what I told myself anyway. Actually, I suppose that the entity that had been piggybacking me wanted its last beer. Anyway, I drank one and went to bed lying in a totally open position on my back my arms spread wide open.

At 3 A.M., while I was in a deep sleep, what sounded like a bolt of lightning struck. It sounded like it was inside the house. It was so loud it woke everyone up and shook the house. The moment my eyes flew open, I saw a black vapor-like being leaving my solar plexus area and heading up through the ceiling and away.

My heart was pounding. I knew exactly what had happened, only I had no idea it would be this dramatic. I jumped up and went to the bathroom. The bleeding had stopped. The smell had gone away. It did not return. I was free.

After My Buddy Left

For a few weeks after this incident, I felt odd. I couldn't shake the feeling of being empty and a little lonely. I also felt unworthy, embarrassed, and weak. I no longer had any doubt that there were such things as demons and dark forces, and I wished I could go back to the time when I didn't know they existed.

But I couldn't go back, so I just had to get out of this somehow. I called Hanna. It seemed that Hanna always knew when we needed a little extra time with her. Usually calls with her lasted all of twenty to thirty seconds—just long enough to get my question answered.

On this day, I called and I could not hold the tears back. They were pouring down my face and constricting my voice.

"Hanna, this is Ginger."

"Yes, Ginger, what can I do for you?"

"Hanna, I just called to tell you that I quit."

I don't know what it was that I thought I was quitting because I hadn't joined anything.

"What's the matter, honey?" Hanna said to me in a soft and tender voice.

"Well, Hanna, I got possessed!"

"So what?" Hanna said.

"Well," I continued, "if I got possessed, it means that I am a bad person."

"It means nothing of the sort," Hanna said incredulously.

"Well, anyway, now that I know that dark forces are real and that I can get possessed, I am too afraid."

"Oh, honey!" Hanna said. "They saw that you were headed for the light, and they wanted to stop you from your mission. That is all that happened!"

Even though this did help make me feel better about myself, I was still afraid. I told Hanna, "Well, I know, Hanna, but I am so afraid of them."

With almost a laugh in her voice she said, "Afraid? Afraid of the dark forces! Honey, don't you know they are just veenies!"

"Weenies?!" (I understood her German accent, and she had meant weenies). That made me laugh.

"Yes, just veenies!" she said. "And they will use your fear against you to stop you from your mission."

Weenies stop me from my mission? No way!

Again my brilliant teacher had given my mind a constructive place to go as I faced a life where weenies were real.

I was giggling now. I felt better. Hanna was giggling with me.

"Hanna," I said, "I learned a lot of lessons from this."

"You and many others," Hanna said.

I was referring to having judgmental and mean thoughts when I realized that someone else was possessed. Now that I had my turn, I shuttered to think of what would have become of my life had Hanna not stopped to free me and then help me to understand that it wasn't me, the real self, that was evil.

She helped me understand that there were a number of things going on, none of which was that I was "bad" or "evil." Perhaps I had unknowingly invited the dark forces in by allowing my anger and my behavior (drinking too much and too often) to get me out of balance, thereby creating a weakness in my energy field. A weakness in one's energy field creates an opportunity for the dark forces to attach.

Or perhaps it was that the dark forces were attracted to my light and wanted it for themselves. All souls really do crave the light, no matter how misguided or lost.

Hanna let me know that my real Self was still intact and in good favor with God, and it would always be that way, no matter what.

Boogies

Through Hanna's teachings and my own experiences, I learned a great deal about the "boogies," or "spooks" as we affectionately call them. Hanna called them dark forces and demons. I learned that they are real, for one thing. And I learned that there are many different types of dark forces or negative entities, most of which are created by our own negative thinking, speaking, and acting in unloving ways.

I learned that poltergeists (house ghosts), disincarnate spirits, and demons are all lost souls up to different types of mischief or wanderings.

Regardless of why they are still hanging out in this dimension, they don't belong here and cannot progress as souls while trapped in this dimension. This dimension is for beings with bodies. The only way we can help them is to send them to the light. It is never appropriate to let them "hang out." They are trapped on the earth plane.

They don't realize that they can seek their own enlightenment. This can only be gained through God and the light, not through humanity and third dimensional reality; therefore, we command them to leave. We do this in the name of Jesus, and tell them, "Follow the Light," or "Follow Jesus to the light," or "Go with God to the Light." You can use whatever phrase is most comfortable to you. We command them with love. They are our unenlightened brothers. They are a part of the whole of which we are a part. It is to our benefit as well as to theirs to see to it that they make it, if we possibly can.

Chapter 10

Lessons Learned

I lost a little bit of my cockiness after this possession incident. I started to take the work more seriously and to make it my business to educate myself better.

I went to Hanna's summer retreat every year except one over the course of twelve years. I did Level 1 & 2 over and over again because that's all she offered. Each time I went, I learned so much. I couldn't hear the material too much. Each time, I seemed to understand it on a deeper level. Each time, she presented new information in addition to the regular teachings.

I found it fascinating and yet aggravating that most of our sicknesses are caused by our own ignorance. I found myself asking, "Why doesn't anyone tell us this?"

Little articles in obscure corners of the newspaper do tell us many of the things we need to know to stay well but they are overshadowed by advertisements to the contrary.

Some of Hanna's bold statements were shocking. "White sugar and white flour are bleached with lead," she said. "The molecule of lead is the same size as a calcium molecule, and a growing body will accept the lead molecule instead of the calcium molecule. This can contribute to behavioral and growth problems. It can be a part of ADD (Attention Deficit Disorder) and ADHD (Attention Deficit Hyperactivity Disorder)."

Hanna also insisted that "aspartame is a brain poison, so is MSG" (monosodium glutamate). Yet, there are tons of products on the market that use both of these.

Dioxin is another toxin that causes all kinds of havoc in the body, but it is in products that we spray on our lawns as an herbicide so we will have nice fluffy grass. Then we let our kids roll around in it. White paper products such as coffee filters and tampons are bleached with dioxin.

Hanna told us that sodium fluoride is a poison that can make the immune system sluggish and is involved in many sicknesses, yet it is in most commercial grade toothpaste. She found sodium fluoride to be devastating to the kidneys and thought that anyone on kidney dialysis was surely the victim of this trend. She also felt that the rise in thyroid disorders was greatly due to this toxin, as well as to mercury toxicity.

She was also horrified that mercury, an extremely toxic metal, was used in dental fillings. She was incredulous at the notion that the only place mercury is not toxic is in the mouth. She told us not to just believe her, ask our dentist how they had to handle a mercury spill or a sodium fluoride spill in their office. Sure enough, she was right, they are required to put on the gloves, masks, and aprons, and they handle it and dispose of it as the toxic, lethal substance that it is.

She was convinced that mercury toxicity was involved in most shaking disorders such as Parkinson's, Multiple Sclerosis, and Lou Gherig's.

It is incredible how these toxins are setting up the environment that supports sickness in the body. Much of our exposure to chemical toxicity occurs inside our own homes. We spray chemicals on the lawn, on the floor, on the windows, on our hair, and in the air. We plug chemicals into the wall so our house will smell better.

The liver has the job to tell the body what to do with all of these chemicals and must do most of the breaking down of them.

The liver can handle only so much before it just can't break down any more junk. Then, it shuttles the toxins off and stores them in some dangerous and unnatural places, like a thyroid, a pancreas, a thymus gland, or a kidney.

By understanding the energetic effects of these chemicals on our body, I understood that chemicals, heavy metals, and environmental toxins were of a vibration that set up the environment in which worms and parasites thrive.

It was Hanna's belief that worms and parasites were almost always involved in diseases. When Hanna first came out with this information, she was thought to be a total kook. We Americans were insulted. We are clean people, we bathe everyday, and we can't have worms!

A Healthy Kitchen

Hanna reminded us that we couldn't afford to live under the illusion that we could do whatever we wanted to our bodies and then go to the medical community and demand a quick fix pill. Her philosophy was, "God helps those who help themselves."

I was learning to help myself. I learned so much about how to have a healthier home. I became aware that bacteria in the kitchen and in food could cause stomach flu and food poisoning. Hanna loved apple cider vinegar and said to use it for bacterial infections because it kills many kinds of bacteria. It can even be sipped, diluted, used to wipe counters, or used for a fruit and vegetable cleaner.

Hanna also told us that we needed some salt in our diet, as every cell of our body requires it. She went so far as to say that salt is Christ's vibration, and only forces of the darkness would want to take it away from us! She further said that a salt-free diet could cause strokes. She taught that real salt has about eighty-eight minerals in it and that table salt was reduced down to one mineral—sodium chloride (with magnesium added for easy pouring). She did think that the body had too much of this (sodium chloride).

She gave us our real butter back. She said that there are certain fats in real butter that body needs in order to work properly. Margarine, she said, is processed with nickel which is a catalyst for tumors. So, not only are we eliminating something we need (linoleic acid) when we avoid butter, we're adding something detrimental to our diet when we substitute margarine.

She would shake her head at low-fat products because so much processing has to be done to most of them that the chemicals we are getting from the processing is usually much harder on the body than the fats that occur naturally.

Proper Food Combining

Hanna taught us that proper food combination was of the utmost importance.

"It isn't what you eat; it's what you digest. Foods eaten in the wrong combination will make you tired and fat and sick," she would say.

Hanna was fond of saying, "Your food should give you energy. You eat to get energy to do your work. If eating makes you tired, then you are not getting the benefit from the food. So why eat it?"

There are many books written on this subject, and Hanna wrote about it in many of her books.

How Does Prayer Affect the Energy Field of Food?

Hanna taught us that organic food was wonderful as long as we weren't angry, arguing, or cursing over the food when we were preparing it. She said that it would be better to eat processed food that we had prayed over and that had been cooked by a happy cook rather than organic food that we argued over.

The reason for this is that food absorbs the energy of the person who prepares it. Then we ingest that vibration. That is why we do well to keep our cooks happy!

We should say a blessing over our food because gratitude is so uplifting it enhances the energy of the food. It is honoring to nature to thank nature for its part in the process of giving its life to sustain and support ours. We take this energy into our bodies, and the nourishment goes clear to the soul!

Our Bodies Are Electric and Magnetic

Hanna felt that the kitchen was the heart of the home. To have a happy and healthy home, make sure there is a happy and healthy kitchen.

Hanna taught us that the human body has an electromagnetic energy field and that women are more magnetic in nature and men were more electric. That's why, she said, in general, women who had all electric kitchens were not the happiest cooks.

She said that all the different sources of electricity in the kitchen—the toaster, the refrigerator, the can opener, the electric stove, and so on—bombard our electromagnetic fields. This can cause us to be out of balance "electromagnetically," which can make us feel depressed, tired, and drained.

She believed that gas stoves were better for the vibration of the food and for the cook. She did not like microwaves for numerous reasons. She described how it doesn't cook the food evenly and consequently did not kill the parasite trichinosis. She also believed that microwaves destroyed the vibration of food.

She said that microwaves were harder on men than on woman because of the male's electric nature. This can cause a man to be irritated, disgruntled, and/or out of sorts. She believed that men often didn't want to be around when a microwave was in use, even though it wasn't a conscious thought.

She said to women, "If you want to get a divorce, don't go pay a fancy lawyer all that money. Just get a microwave!"

There was so much information. There was so much to learn. I was constantly amazed at the new doors that were being opened in my own consciousness.

Harvey, the Healer Who Could See into the Body

Besides introducing me to Hanna, Belva Bloomer also introduced me to the most fascinating guy. His name was Harvey Bevier. Harvey had the gift of being able to see into bodies. He had "x-ray vision." When he was in the war, he would go up in the airplanes, and he could see through the trees, foliage, houses, and hiding places. From high above, he could see the enemy through buildings, trees, shelters or wherever they were hiding. Even the military was aware of his great abilities and used him for this talent.

The good side of this is that he eventually used this to help heal thousands of people. He could see the bones, ligaments, tendons, and nerves, and he could see where the energy wasn't flowing properly. He could also somehow tell what caused this trauma. He would then adjust the bones and free up the energy flow.

Harvey was a holy man. He was small in structure and strong as an ox. I saw him lift men who were 6'6" tall, and he couldn't have been more than 5'8" himself. He wasn't as old as Hanna but he wasn't a spring chicken either. They were cronies. They had a mutual admiration and respect for each other.

He would see people for whatever money they wanted to offer him, and many times it was for one dollar or five dollars or ten. He helped many poor people, both financially poor and those who were poor of spirit. His work was amazing, and I always got good results.

I would go directly to see Harvey when I arrived in Colorado—even before going to Hanna's Retreat. I would take my friends, my family, whoever. We all loved going to see Harvey, even though his adjustments were sometimes painful. At the Retreat there was always a three-hour break from class on Saturday. This is when we would get in our second visit to Harvey. Then, after the class was over and before we left town, we would go for our third time. This was the scenario that Harvey advised to fine tune the adjustments.

Harvey was a wonderful man and as many such healers, including Hanna, was the subject of jealousy and gossip by those who attempt to build up their own egos by putting others down.

Upon returning from one of the Saturday breaks, I heard such a commotion from some women who were at Hanna's for the first time and who had also just had their first Harvey visit. Although they had been amazed by being worked on by Harvey and had thought that he was wonderful, there was one of these "all-knowing" women in the class who was telling everyone that people came back from Harvey's "possessed."

Since this woman had been at Hanna's a number of times the women who were there for the first time thought that this person must know something. They were all very upset. Their experience had told them otherwise, but now they didn't even trust their own experience. They were also freaked out from the thought that they may be possessed and not know it.

I was furious when I heard what this woman had said. I was angry with her for speaking irreverently about such a wonderful person and for frightening these women. My companions and I decided to go to Hanna with this problem.

Hanna Teaches Us Another Subtle Lesson

Hanna was not going to put up with this gossip. She thanked us for telling her and said that she would handle it. I was surprised that she didn't walk over to the woman and whack her. Actually, I was hoping for that. There was so much upset in the room because half of the people there had been to see Harvey at some time or another.

This woman was saying that she was the incarnation of somebody important. After all, she had been around Hanna's for a while. That must mean that she was legitimate.

With so much upset in the room, Hanna needed to handle it for more than just one or two people. A master teacher is always teaching. She waited the few minutes until class resumed. Then she said in the most cheerful, happy voice, "Who knows Harvey?"

There was much apprehension in the room. Those who had been shaken up the most didn't know whether or not to admit that they had been to Harvey's in case the gossip lady was right. Hands were not going up. The class was sheepishly looking around to see who would raise their hands.

Again Hanna said, "Who here knows Harvey?"

Slowly, half the hands in the room went up.

Hanna beamed. She looked up to the heavens, put her hands together as though in prayer, and said with so much love and respect in her voice, "Harvey is a holy man!"

That was it. She didn't say another word. She didn't have to. The energy in the room calmed down, and we got back to the class material. We all went to see Harvey on our way out of town and again when we returned in the subsequent years.

The Ego Wants the Credit

There were many intriguing interactions that I witnessed with Hanna. In each interaction, there were so many lessons available to me and whoever else cared to learn.

Once again, I was at the retreat with a couple of my friends to attend a Level 2 class. I don't remember what I was doing in the classroom area, as class was not in session at that time, but I did look up to see a beautiful woman in the full dress of her ethnic tradition walk through the door. She continued into the dining room and living area.

I simply noted her presence. There were always so many fascinating people that showed up around Hanna.

Within a few minutes, I went in the living area to find my friends Gilda and Tommy distracted and distressed. Tommy had been seriously ill for a long time and required regular periods of rest. He was resting on a sofa.

I asked them what was wrong. Gilda said that the woman and her attitude had barged in on their space and demanded to know what was going on here.

Gilda and Tommy were totally confused. Did she mean, "What was going on with them?" Or, did she mean, "What was going on at the retreat?"

They questioned her.

"At the retreat," she replied abruptly.

Apparently, the woman indicated to them that she was "a healer" and didn't need the beginner class. She seemed insulted that they failed to realize how truly advanced she was.

Tommy and Gilda both had the same reaction. "Oh, no, not one of those."

They both were aware that this was an ego display, and they knew this meant trouble.

It only took one peacock ego to get Hanna fired up. Where one show-off struts, there are often a few more, and none of us was up for dealing with that kind of energy. We had come to be with each other and to be with Hanna. We had come to learn, to rest, and to experience the wonderful energy around Hanna and her work. We did not want to have to battle the energy of a know-it-all.

I noticed on the breaks on Thursday and Friday that this woman was always following Hanna around, apparently wanting special recognition from her. It seemed that she was not interested in how Hanna chose to teach. She seemed only to want to be recognized as the "healer" that she claimed to be. Hanna was not giving her the kind of recognition that she wanted.

On Saturday morning (the day before the end of the session), the woman appeared in the classroom, while class was going on, with all of her luggage. She was leaving, and she wanted the entire class to know it. Her timing was interesting. Hanna didn't miss this.

She had wanted Hanna's attention, and now she was going to get it.

"Where are you going?"

Hanna glanced over to the side of the room to see the woman leaving.

"I'm leaving," the woman announced to the room.

"Why are you leaving?" Hanna questioned knowingly.

"Well, Hanna, you said I had a blood clot!"

This explanation did not make sense to any of us.

"So what?" Hanna said.

Hanna was such a loving teacher. She was going to use every moment available to her to reach her student.

Hanna continued, "Well, if you are leaving, then come over here, and let me work on your blood clot."

The Energy "Hook"

The woman came over and sat in Hanna's tall chair in front of the room. As she was settling into the seat, she looked directly at me trying to "hook" me into her drama. I knew that energy manipulation and was not going to allow it.

"No way!" I thought. I turned my head and continued to think, "You are not going to get any agreement from me that Hanna is a kook and you are the smart one. No way."

The ego feeds off drama. If it can't find drama, it will create it. The more agreement it can get from outside sources, the more energy it has to run its game.

I glanced around the room to watch the others avert her gaze as she tried to reel us in to her upset. No one was going for it.

Like Energy Attracts Like Energy

Hanna used a little board to dissolve clots. It had black strap molasses and a magnet in it. Her theory for using this was that the iron in the molasses would attract the iron in the clotted blood. The magnet would help dissolve them.

Hanna began her work. She was working around the heart. I could see that the woman's energy was beginning to shift although she was fighting hard not to totally surrender. She put up a good battle. I could see the tears in her eyes.

I had seen it with others on whom Hanna had worked. When the energy around the heart is freed up a flood of tears follow.

She successfully fought back the tears. Hanna worked on a few more areas and then said abruptly, "Done. Now, what's it going to be? You staying or you're leaving?"

Hanna seemed unattached.

The woman seemed not to be ready for this question.

"Well, I guess I'm still going," she said in an uncommitted tone. Then she walked over to the door where her luggage sat waiting. It was my feeling that she wanted Hanna to beg her to stay. Work for it. But Hanna didn't play games.

"Wait here," Hanna commanded.

The woman waited. The class watched. Not a sound was heard. Upon returning to the classroom, Hanna handed her a stack of cash.

"Here is your money back," Hanna said.

The woman was taken aback. She softened. At any point she could have dropped her guard and just sat down, and the class would have continued with all of us having learned valuable lessons from this exchange.

"But Hanna, you haven't even had time to cash my check. I don't need this back. I was here a few days, I don't need it all back."

"Take it," Hanna said, "and have a nice life."

Everyone, except Hanna, was stunned. The woman opened the door and left. Her eyes seemed to cry indignant tears, from what I could feel.

Hanna turned right back to the class and said something like, "Let them leave. Give them their money back. But heal them first, before they go."

She took up teaching where she left off and never mentioned the woman again.

I thought about that woman many times. It was my feeling that her real chance at being a "true healer" was given to her by Hanna being willing to let her go. What a service Hanna had rendered by letting her go, letting her meet herself on the road back home. I often wonder if she used the opportunity to really get it. I hope so. I had benefited tremendously from Hanna exposing my stuff—my ego and my weaknesses in front of a packed seminar room. I hoped this woman would get it, too.

The saints and holy people seem to have a way of burning the "crap," the "unworkable" junk, right out of us. Thank God.

But What Makes a Saint a Saint?

I was on a good path with Hanna as my teacher in my life. I felt that I was being watched over by God. It felt good. Then one day I went over to Lee's house, and she showed me this beautiful book-like magazine that a friend had given her. It had a deep red color cover and a photo of the most incredible looking East Indian woman. I flipped absentmindedly through the magazine. I liked the energy of it. It felt holy and sacred.

I found myself petting that book, putting it down, and picking it up again, flipping through it, petting it, and putting it down again.

I had no idea that I was about to meet yet another wonderful teacher. Her name was Gurumayi. She was about my age, and she was supposedly "enlightened." She was from India but was spending a good deal of time in the United States.

I was later told that the Eastern people do not wait for their holy people to die to declare them saints. They recognized saints, holy people, and gurus during their lifetime.

In the East, it is common knowledge that a real guru is not good news for the ego. I suppose that was what God had in mind when he sent her into my life. I wonder if she and others like her ever ask God to change His mind and throw that student back for some other teacher to deal with?

I had Hanna, so I didn't need Gurumayi or any other holy people or teachers. But she was so compelling, so mesmerizing. What was it about her? The essence of love and a deep stillness seemed to pour from her being. Just studying her photo, I felt calmer and more peaceful.

I put the magazine down, and I forgot about her.

Now looking back, it was at that time that my life seemed to accelerate—the changes in my life accelerated. I guess the good Lord realized that my ego wasn't going to push over easily. It was going to require heavy artillery to combat it.

Chapter 11

Shattered

The Dark Night of the Soul

December 1989 started the period I now call my "shattering." To me, shattering is a sign of blessing, because you get to rediscover your real self. But, at the time, shattering did not feel like a blessing; it felt like a very long and painful beating.

My life fell apart seemingly overnight. My relationship shattered, and my business was shattering. My store in New Orleans was failing faster than should have been possible posing an alarming financial drain on my other store that was located in the Florida panhandle. My business seemed destined to collapse under the weight of the financial pressure. Everything about my external and most of my internal life was coming apart.

My Financial Shattering

When money doesn't work in our lives, when we are broke and heavily in debt, life can look extra frightening. I had never been more frightened in my life.

I had a talent for selling merchandise in my store. I was good at many things in my business, but I was not good at "the business of business." In fact, I was ignorant about what it really took to make a business work from the financial perspective.

I had moved my New Orleans store (nothing to do with Hanna's work) from a shopping mall into an old and popular section of town called the French Quarter. My new location was two blocks off the beaten path—the cardinal sin of retail. A location two blocks off the beaten path was two blocks too far. We didn't last three months. Plus, during that time, we were robbed five times. Four of these times one of my employees or I actually watched the robbers carry an entire rack of the most expensive sportswear out the door. There was nothing I could do but call the police. There was nothing they could do when they arrived an hour or so later.

Apparently, this sort of thing happened all the time. The streets in the New Orleans French Quarter are all one-way streets. So, the robbers would ride their bikes or flee on foot going the opposite direction of the one way streets. This was very effective since the police cars would be going in the wrong direction to catch them.

Another time, there was a burglary in the middle of the night. The massive plate glass window was broken, and money and merchandise were stolen. If this wasn't bad enough, the policeman who showed up to write the report acted like he was on drugs. He did as much damage as the robbers, breaking my neon sign in the name of clearing a path.

I felt like a victim. Everything seemed to be going wrong. I had to look long and hard to see where I had participated in creating this situation from which I now found myself suffering. I really did not want to tell the truth about this one, but how could I avoid it and not have this lesson follow me around for the rest of this incarnation?

I had to admit to myself that I had done something wrong. My personal integrity had been sorely lacking when I had opened that store. I knew that there was a moratorium on T-shirt shops in the French Quarter, which meant that they wouldn't approve opening another one. I justified it to myself that my shop was different. I changed the name of my shop to drop the "T-shirt." Well now it really was different because now nobody could tell what kind of store it was supposed to be. This was foolish.

How in the world did I expect to succeed when I built the future of my business on a foundation lacking in integrity? I knew better. It was a formula for failure. I tested universal law, and universal law revealed itself again.

This "shattering" was like a tornado. It swooped in, wreaked havoc and left, leaving a trail of devastation, or was it? Was this perhaps the Cosmic Cleaning Committee? This shattering force, this energy that had entered my life had a mind of its own. Surely it was being directed by a higher power which seemed to be looking for the things in my life that were weak or flawed or lacking in integrity. It found them.

I lost my apartment, I lost a store, I lost my relationship, I lost my dogs and some of my friends. I lost my dignity, and I almost lost my sanity. I was so completely shattered and lonely. I couldn't face anyone. I was embarrassed about the desperate place I was in. I was so humiliated and angry about being left. I felt abandoned both personally and professionally. (The ego despises looking bad or pathetic.)

At the time, I couldn't figure out what had gone wrong. In retrospect, it wasn't that things had gone wrong. It was that things were going right for me. One of my friends told me, during one of my worst times, "It's not that your life is falling apart, it's that it's falling together." I had to shatter. It was imperative that I give up trying or even wanting to put my life back to the way it was.

From the experience of "shattering," we have a real opportunity for awakening and meeting ourselves at a place we've never been before. We have the chance to discover the true nature of our reality, ourselves, our spirits, and the depth of our beings. We have the precious opportunity to glimpse the reality of our Oneness with All that Is, our love for our fellow being, and our devotion to God.

When we crawl through the dark tunnel where we, many times, can see no light at all, we get to discover the true nature of Faith.

When we glimpse the light at the end of the tunnel, we begin to discover the true nature of Grace.

When we experience the depth of pain and sorrow and grief that comes with shattering, we become mystified with the knowing that we were able to feel the depth of that pain. This leads us to the understanding that if we can feel this new depth of pain, then we will also be able to feel a new depth of love.

No matter how hard I tried, I would not be able to put the pieces of my life back together again. I would find out who I really was, at a much deeper level.

I had found out years earlier that I wasn't my fancy watch, but now I was finding out that I wasn't my beloved relationship, and I wasn't my credit cards or my business.

Lee was my salvation, my most committed ally, my best support, and my link to sanity. I called her sometimes ten times a day. Each time she would listen to me and help me through this incredible dark night of the soul. She did this by patiently listening, not "agreeing," "judging," or "getting into the drama" with me. Lee didn't run from my sorrow and my pain, which could be brutal to be around, I'm sure. Many of my other friends had chosen the more fun half of this broken up couple. I wasn't the fun half.

By talking things out, I was able to remember that life was good, God was close, and that I was a good and loving person, worthy of being loved. Lee reminded me that all of these trials were just lessons for my soul's benefit. With that context, I could go on another moment, another day.

The hardest part lasted six solid months, day in and day out. My soul was in torment.

I had to learn to live one minute at a time because I could not see anything in the future that was going to make it all right. I could not see any light at the end of the tunnel. I was miserable, out of my mind miserable. And I was broke and alone.

Well, I wasn't totally alone, because three times I heard a male voice say out loud to me, "Oh, ye of little faith." The voice was always kind of laughing. I never was.

I Hit the Bottom in a Daydream

I didn't have faith. I had pain. I remember daydreaming my pain. I owned a car that had a sun roof. In the daydream, I was driving down St. Charles Avenue in New Orleans with my car windows down and my sun roof open. It was a bright sunny spring day. A gunman approached my car. As he held his gun to my chest, ready to pull the trigger, I looked into his face, and I said, "Thank you."

The pathetic nature of this little daydream was shocking to me. I knew I had to do something, but I didn't know what.

Surrender!

One day, I had it. I couldn't go a step farther on my own. I fell to my knees. I surrendered. I clasped my hands together and closed my eyes so tightly. I said aloud to God, "Okay, okay, God, I surrender. I surrender! I will do whatever you want me to do."

I was weeping. Again and again I repeated the words, "I surrender, God. I surrender." I have no idea what you want of me but I am listening now. I will do whatever you want me to do, I will go wherever you want me to go, I will be with whomever you choose, but please Lord, you know how hardheaded I am, so make the message real loud!"

Awakening

I cried my eyes out. I surrendered to the will of God, and then I surrendered again. I found that I would have to do this on a regular basis. Doing it for the first time, fully, was so freeing. Something happened in those moments. Something released, and I awakened to the understanding that I had turned my life over completely in service for God, without conditions or stipulations.

My life did not just become a bed of roses overnight. It was a daily battle to keep going, but now I believed that there was light at the end of this tunnel.

I really wanted to do Hanna's work, but I knew that I could not possibly support myself from this alone, and that would present a problem. I had even made a statement to a group who had come to my house to see a visiting practitioner. "I would love to be able to make a living doing Hanna's work, but that is not realistic. Everyone knows you can't make a living selling herbs."

As the group was leaving my apartment, one of the men gave me a little piece of paper. He told me not to read it then but to put it on my pillow and read it before I went to bed. Although I did not seek advice from this man, I put it on my pillow anyway.

Before going to bed I opened the note.

It read, "Do what you love, and the money will follow."

The note uplifted me but I knew it wasn't realistic. Still, I repeated those words over and over, like a mantra. I knew I would never be able to support myself in the healing arts, but repeating that phrase, "Do what you love, and the money will follow," made me feel better.

In the meantime, I was the one in the most need of healing. I was working on myself and things were changing. The most fascinating things were beginning to happen. As the old relationships and ways of doing things were falling away, a new energy was coming in. There was a sweetness entering that would replace the voids, a softness that would caress me. As one thing would be taken away, something new and more fitting would take its place.

Colorado

When I went to Colorado that summer for summer school, I visited my college friend Chris Farrugia, and she introduced me to LaRae. My life started healing and took a happy turn. I stayed in Colorado longer than I had planned, and then LaRae came back with me to Florida and helped me make it through a tough summer in my business and a tough time in my life. We both ended up going back to Colorado once the tourist season was over in Florida. There was no sense in my staying in Florida. There was almost no business during the winter.

With the loss of the New Orleans store, my Florida store was caving in to the financial stress, and now I was going to lose it too. It was only a matter of time.

Going to Colorado for a long winter saved my life. LaRae had a beautiful new house in the mountains, and I had the solitude that I needed and the time to think, to rest, to listen, and to just "be." This was the kind of time that I had seldom had before. The air up there was so pure, and I was starting to feel my "life force" returning to me.

It was during that time that I would go over to Hanna's house a few times a week. She would give me work to do. She was teaching me to do what we called "saliva work" (a form of reading the body's energy field, psychometrically from a distance using the person's saliva). She gave me work, and she gave me instructions. She would let me help her in little ways, probably because she knew how pitifully broke I was. She knew I needed her.

Week after week, I went to her house. While we worked, she would listen to the problems I was having with my business back in Florida and with my life. She listened and she counseled me. Mostly though, she watched, guided, and befriended me.

While spending this amount of time with her, I was able to observe her life. I guess one of the most powerful lessons I would learn was that being Hanna wasn't easy or glamorous. I had considered Hanna to be a holy person and maybe even a living saint from the moment that I had met her, but I guess I thought she came out of the womb that way.

Spending private time with her, I came to realize that she had lessons to learn, just like everyone else. Her life was a human one. But I noticed that even with her human frailties and her flaws, her heart was engaged in her work, always.

Hanna and Her Daughter Lisa

One day, I got a phone call from my mother. She knew Lisa's story because Hanna would share this in the seminar.

Hanna's youngest daughter Lisa had undergone a life of torment and sickness as the result of a polio vaccination. My mother told me that there was an article in the newspaper that said that the government was extending the deadline for lawsuits to be filed against it. It was for people who had been injured or who had a child who had died or had been injured from the polio vaccination. They had extended the deadline another day.

I practically flew over to Hanna's house. I was thrilled with the news. Hanna was not thrilled; she was sad, distraught, overwhelmed, the horror of the memories of those earlier days rushing back to her.

"I cannot do that," she said. "I would not know where to start."

"I will do it for you, Hanna. I have the time, and I will make the calls and figure out how to do it," I told her.

"Okay," she said.

I made a few phone calls and found out the names of the lawyers who were handling these cases. There was some rule that if the persons filing the lawsuit won their case against the government, the government would have to pay the attorney.

I was relieved to find this wonderful attorney. I was relieved that it wouldn't cost any money because I knew Hanna would win the case.

The attorney told me that due to the number of people responding to the deadline extension, it had again been extended. Now we had an additional three days to put our case together.

I went to work. This meant that I had to dig up every available record of Lisa's young life. I would have to provide school records, medical records, and records of the vaccination campaign that year.

I went to work. I made many calls.

At one point, Hanna (who had been listening to me make endless calls tracking down the information that we needed), stopped for a moment, patted me on the back and said, "You are so smart."

I discovered that they didn't even keep records of the vaccinations. They had just lined up all the kids at one of the local schools and gave it to them.

The schools didn't retain records of attendance that far back, although I did get to talk to a man who had been with the school system that long. How would I even prove that Lisa was ever a brilliant student and that this vaccination had ruined her life? Everything would have to be documented by affidavit, except the medical records.

I located the hospital where Lisa's medical records were; however, they weren't going to release them to me. I asked Hanna to take a ride with me to get them. "Take Lisa with you," she said.

"Take Lisa?" I thought. I was appalled. "Lisa is totally not home," I was thinking. "What good will Lisa do me?"

Hanna must have read my thoughts because she said, "Lisa is an adult. She can sign her name. They will release the records to her."

"Lisa is an adult!"

God, I hadn't even thought of that. I knew Lisa had to be around forty-three years old at that time, but Hanna interacted with her as though she was a child. Up to that point, Lisa had never even talked to me except to say, "Go home."

I was nervous driving in the car with Lisa. I didn't know what she might do. After a few minutes, I forgot about Lisa, since she was sitting quietly, staring out the car window. I concentrated on navigating my way to the hospital. I didn't know my way around Boulder very well. Time was of the essence. There was so much to do.

Glancing into my rear view mirror, I saw the police lights and then heard the siren. I had longtime since stopped asking myself the question "What else can go wrong?" because I found out that the Universe had an endless list of answers to that question.

"God, I am so broke, please don't let him give me a ticket," I was praying.

I rolled down my window as the police officer approached the car. "Do you know how fast you were going?" he asked.

Honestly, I did not, but I was sure I was speeding. I couldn't lie. I wouldn't lie. I was going to get a ticket.

"Do you know how many points that is going to cost you on your license?"

He could see that I had a brand new Colorado driver's license, so he could figure that I was ignorant as to the severity of this infraction in Boulder.

Right at that moment, as the police officer was leaning down asking me this important and alarming question, Lisa opened her car door and threw up. I groaned and my stomach lurched. Then she did it again.

He let us go with only a warning. Lisa's timing was so incredible that I started to view her differently. Perhaps somewhere in that tortured head and body there really was an intelligent being. Now I was really grateful for having Lisa with me.

Hanna was right. Lisa could write her name in script, and they let her sign for her own records.

I was amazed at the volume of paperwork that was in her files. We had to drive to several locations to get it all. I was horrified when I read the saga of her life after the vaccine. It all started within seventy-two hours of the vaccination. At first, the symptom was a high fever that lasted too long, and then it was the seizures that have lasted the rest of Lisa's life.

Hanna and her husband, Rudolph, took Lisa to many doctors and made countless trips to the hospital. She was having seizures on a daily basis, and she was slipping off into a dark world. The once brilliant little nine year old was now becoming unrecognizable. She had loved school, and now she was missing a lot of it. It was getting worse. Her mental abilities were failing, and those seizures were wreaking havoc on her little body.

During most of her life, Lisa has lived with multiple daily grand mal seizures. This desperate way of life took its toll. As she got older, the suicide attempts started. Fits of rage consumed her life, and the running away began. She became like an animal. Like a beast. Was this the "mark of the beast"? After the seizures, she would get extremely weak, bringing on a terrible depression.

For the rest of their lives, either Rudolph or Hanna had to sleep in the room with her, due to her nightly seizures.

Hanna was driven by the deep desire to help her child. She studied, researched, and formulated products to try to help Lisa. The medications had their limitations. They were not healing her. This mother was driven by her love for a sick child.

Many of Hanna's formulas were actually created in the search of the healing product for Lisa. One example, the X-40 kit, was created as a direct result of the search. Hanna had realized that the polio vaccination was manufactured from a live virus cultured in a medium from the infected kidney of monkeys and that monkeys carried a deadly retrovirus. Product after product, Hanna tried them all on Lisa. Sometimes there were improvements, but she was never able to totally bring Lisa back from the abyss.

I was shocked at what I learned. Horrified.

We filed the lawsuit. If we won that would mean that the government would provide for Lisa's care for the rest of her life. Rudolph, an eighty-year-old man at this time, told me that if they won the case, he would be able to die in peace. He said that it was the one thing that concerned him the most.

We got every thing filed on time. I felt very optimistic about the case. Hanna told me not to get too anxious because as she said, "They will probably drag this out for years." Again she was right. As of this writing, nine years later, the case is still not settled.

Following Instructions

I learned to follow Hanna's instructions and trust her intuition. Whenever I did what she told me to do, she proved to be right. Whenever I didn't follow her instructions, I found out that she was still right!

Hanna was an instigator. She could really rock the boat or calm the waters, whatever was needed at the moment. When she needed to be hopeful, she was hopeful; when she needed to be powerful, she was powerful. When she needed faith, she was faithful. She was always inspirational.

Ginger, ready to help Hanna.
Madison, Wisconsin seminar, 1997

Hanna teaching. Ginger assisting.

Hanna with Southern Herb, Madison Staff in 1997.
Left to right: Bobbi Brooks, Robin Jeanblanc, Claire
Culbertson, LaRae J. Palo, Noah Tabakin, Hanna
Kroeger, Ginger Bowler, Dan Lautenschlaeger.

Hanna explains her
findings to a student.

Hanna checks the vibration of lettuce.

Hanna demonstrates how to position the hands to send healing prayers.

Photo by Christopher D. Comello

Hanna measures an energy field of the heart.

Ginger holds mic for Hanna.

Photo by Christopher D. Comello

Chapter 12
Teaching and Learning

Somehow through all of this, I thought I should start traveling around teaching seminars on Hanna's work. I don't know where I got such a crazy idea, but I had it in my head that I really knew something and that I should go out in the world and teach this great information. I guess I actually did get some nudging from Hanna. Hanna thought everyone could teach. "You can do it," she would say.

One day she actually told me, "Oh, Ginger, you could talk your way out of a hole!" I guess I thought this was some sort of encouragement. Surely it was a compliment! Anyway, I set out to be a seminar leader.

By now, it was 1991. My sister, Maureen, was my first seminar host. She lived in south Louisiana, and I was living in Colorado at the time. She got a small group together, and I went to teach and preach. I brought about four million dollars worth of merchandise with me, and there were eight people there, including two of my sisters and me. As if that wasn't bad enough, I was awful at presenting Hanna's work, completely awful.

Two of the students knew more about candida albicans overgrowth and the problems associated with it than I had ever hoped to, and that's all they wanted to talk about.

I left there completely traumatized. I never wanted to teach a seminar again. I now knew how truly ignorant I was, and so did some of those folks down the bayou.

The problem was that I had another seminar already scheduled for me by Hanna. It was in Evergreen, Colorado. It might as well have been in Hanna's back yard! Oh, God!

I went back to Colorado, I went back to Hanna's house, and I went to confession. I told her all about it. She told me it was time to prepare better, and she started to help me. Then David, one of her other students, who was a proficient and successful teacher, helped me put my teacher's manual together. I remember telling Hanna that I felt like I was studying for a final exam, and she said, "Yes, the first of many!"

I slid through the Evergreen seminar unscathed. In other words, I survived. I still wanted to teach again.

The Evergreen people were kind and said that they enjoyed the class. They didn't throw anything at me or leave early. The ones who hadn't previously known of Hanna would now go and meet her, now that they knew how close she was. I felt I had gotten my job done. I thought everyone should meet Hanna.

When spring arrived, I moved back to the panhandle of Florida as it was time to open my ailing store for the season again. Off-season, I would continue with a busy travel and teaching schedule.

When I found out that Hanna was tired of working the industry trade shows, I decided that I would do it for her. For years she would go with her husband or one of her employees or students and set up a booth at the various holistic health expos and trade shows. She wanted to show people her products and introduce them to her methods of helping themselves.

I told her business manager my idea. He agreed to let me try my hand at these trade shows. I was experienced at retail sales and loved Hanna's work. I wasn't afraid of hard work, and I thought this opportunity would prove to be somewhat glamorous.

I was so enthusiastic about the opportunity to represent Kroeger Herb Products at the Whole Life Expos, the New Life Expo in New York, and shows such as that. I thought I was in for some real fun, not to say that it wasn't. The fact is I had no idea what personal strength I would have to muster to be good at this.

Trade shows are hard work. The fun part is sharing the "work." What was difficult about these shows was the length of time on your feet in a little tiny booth, answering the same questions over and over, the travel and the logistics of setting up and tearing down a booth, with as many different products as we had.

The glamour quickly wore off, lost somewhere on the late night bus rides to my sister Margaret's house in New Jersey since we couldn't afford a hotel room in New York. (We had arranged with Tom at Kroeger Herb that we would pay for our own accommodations).

LaRae and I did most of the expos and trade shows together, traveling from coast to coast. We would go to New York, Los Angeles, San Diego, New York again, San Francisco, Atlanta, New Orleans, New York again, Miami, Santa Fe, Boston—wherever there was going to be a good turnout for a trade show.

The thing that I loved most about doing the shows was that so many people would come up to our booth and tell us miraculous and heartwarming stories about Hanna and how she had helped them or had healed someone in their family. This was always the kind of motivation and inspiration that we would need to keep going.

At these trade shows, I would usually apply to be a speaker, and they would always give me a spot somewhere to speak. I had a lot of nerve—or something. So I was getting quite a bit of experience in speaking to groups.

I always preferred it when Hanna would come to do the speaking. She did attend many of our trade shows. That would always make our job back at the booth a lot easier, as Hanna would go and do a one- or two-hour talk and get the folks all riled up! They would be so excited about whatever she said that they would come and swamp us at the booth, and we would be busy, busy the rest of the show.

The Teacher Throws the Student into the Fire

One season, we had one expo after another. It was a good year. The shows were very large and very well attended, and Hanna was coming to speak at quite a few of them.

We were at the New Life Expo in New York. On Friday, she presented a fantastic one-hour lecture which was packed with attendees. On Saturday, she gave a three-hour workshop which had also gone very well. Hanna and I were both feeling great and happy as we headed out of the seminar room on our way back to the booth.

We were walking rather briskly down the hallway going back to the booth when she turned and casually, but with a hint of laughter in her voice, said to me, "I'm not going to California next week."

"What?" I said in disbelief. "You have to go to California."

We had another big expo, and she was scheduled to speak. There was always a good turnout in California for Hanna. She couldn't back out now.

"I'm not going," she said again smiling at me as we walked side by side.

"You are going to speak," she said to me matter-of-factly.

"No, Hanna, no...." Now I was whimpering, begging. "You have to come. I can't speak instead of you. Everyone is expecting you, not me. They will be very upset. Please, don't do that to me."

"You will be fine," she said.

"But what will I tell them? Why will I say you are not coming?" I whined.

"Tell them the truth. My husband is not well, and I am staying home with him."

That was it. End of discussion. She was going to throw me into the fire, and I was going to die of embarrassment there.

I calmed myself by telling myself that she would change her mind. In case she didn't, I had a back up plan—coercion. When I got back home, I called Tom Brown, her manager. He could talk some sense into her. He would be able to convince her that she really wanted to go.

All Tom could say was, "Oh, boy".

"Oh, Tom, please talk her into it. I'll get eaten alive there."

"I'll see what I can do," he said.

I felt hopeful. Tom was such a grounded person. He had a wonderful head on his shoulders. He was firm but professional, and he had always been so up front with me. I knew he would do what he could. Hanna respected him, as he did her. He seemed to be the one who would always follow her instructions and orders even when it was painful for him to do so, even when he thought she was making a mistake. So she trusted him, as did I. If anybody could make it happen, he could.

Tuesday rolled around, and it was time to pack for California. The phone rang. It was Tom.

"Ginger," he said. "I have bad news. She's not going."

"Oh, God, Tom, she has to go. I cannot stand up in front of a room full of people and say whoops it's me, Hanna couldn't make it. I can't,

Tom. Everyone will walk out."

"I know," Tom said, fully appreciating what would happen. "Will you be all right doing it?"

"Yeah," I said, resigned.

"Good," he said. "Call me when you get back, and let me know how it went."

"Thanks, Tom," I said with a sigh.

"Oh, you're welcome," he said knowingly.

Tom was so stable. He had to be. There were plenty of opportunities with Hanna and the different circumstances around Hanna to make him a complete fruitcake. Somehow, he seemed to be able to maintain his stability and sense of humor through it all. Sometimes this meant doing things that he would rather not have to do (like telling me I was going to have to do this talk), but he did follow Hanna's instructions, like it or not.

One day, years later, I asked him how he was able to do it all those years. He said it was because he truly loved and respected Hanna. I knew that was the truth.

I went to that California expo with a knot in my stomach. Before the lecture was to begin, I called Hanna. I always called Hanna before all of my talks and seminars so that she could be with me during that time. I knew she had the ability to astral project, as I had asked her that question years earlier. So, whether or not she astral traveled to survey and monitor the class or whether she just went into a prayerful state, I always felt connected with her after the call.

When it was time for the workshop to begin, I went to the front of the room, and in a very firm and hurried voice I blurted out,

"Hi, folks. My name is Ginger Bowler. Hanna Kroeger cannot be here this evening, so I am going to lead the seminar. For any of you who do not want to stay, I completely understand and you should go to the room monitor at the back of the room, and she will refund your entire fee."

I had not taken a breath or even paused for a moment in that statement. I said it as though it was all one sentence.

I waited as about a third of the room left. I was actually thrilled. Only a third left. This meant two-thirds of the room stayed. Some of them expressed deep disappointment that Hanna was not there, but I think those who stayed understood fully that no one was more disappointed than I. They were a good class, and I got my job done.

Hanna was gleeful. Tom was relieved. I was satisfied.

The Parrot

While assisting Hanna at seminars, I was getting loads of practice trying to explain what Hanna meant by certain things. I was always trying to find ways to make things simpler for people so they could understand her. This started out very unofficially. My sister Nora and I went to Hanna's retreat. It was 1989, and during the time when Hanna did not have helpers in the classroom. It was also at the time when the classes were still conducted in her living room area.

The class was small, perhaps twenty-five students. Nora and I sat on the floor because this would enable us to be closer to Hanna in order for us to soak up everything she said and to bathe in her energy field. Hanna was hoarse when the class started, and, as it went on, she got progressively more hoarse.

Her voice was soft to start with, and her thick accent was a challenge in and of itself. Her hoarseness, as well as the addition of all these unfamiliar terms and product names, caused a constant buzz in the room.

"What did she say?"

"What is she saying?"

"Hanna, can you repeat that?"

Hanna's tired voice was already so overworked. I started turning around and repeating almost everything she would say. I would say it very quickly and in a loud enough voice that all could hear. Then, I would glance quickly at Hanna to make sure she wasn't going to throw something at me. Then it would start all over again.

We got through that section of the class, and it was going to be time for the outdoor herb walk.

"Wow, this is going to be tough. If people can't hear Hanna in the house, they will never be able to hear her outside," I was thinking. I knew it would be good to go outside anyway. It was a beautiful morning.

Before Hanna dismissed the class to go outside, she motioned to my sister and me. Nora and I scooted closer to her. We were still seated on the floor. We were both looking up into her face. She looked into my eyes and said to me in a raspy, weakened tone, "You will be my voice."

"Okay," I said rather sheepishly.

I immediately looked into my sister's questioning eyes. I had chills running up the back of my neck. Apparently, she did too.

"What just happened?" Nora asked in wonderment.

"I don't know." I said, "Did you feel that too?"

"God, I have chills. The hair is standing up on my arms," Nora said.

"She just wants me to repeat what she says on the herb walk," I said. "Yeah, right!" Nora said.

We looked at each other, raised our eyebrows at each other, and, with a chuckle, headed out into the warm Colorado sun.

It would be another few years before I would work with her in any kind of official or even semiofficial capacity.

Filming Hanna's Video

From this time on, I was always trying to find ways to make things simpler for people so that they could understand Hanna's work more easily. One of the ways I did this was by producing a video of her hands-on healing techniques. This was quite a challenge to get Hanna to agree to get in front of television cameras and "perform." This just wasn't her nature. I had to be creative with this project. I came up with the solution of having a studio audience made up of "real people" who were interested in her teachings. That way, when she saw them, the cameras would disappear, and she would be teaching and helping people.

This worked. She saw people in need of help and jumped right to the chance. The studio crew was really having to scramble because Hanna wasn't following the outline that I had given them. The teleprompter was cueing her for the next thing on the agenda, and she totally ignored it. I knew that was going to happen. I had tried to tell the studio crew that there was no way that she was going to stick to any format, but they didn't like that answer. Everyone goes by an outline or script.

Since they seemed as hardheaded as Hanna, my brother Mike and I typed a script of all the things that she should go over (sometime in the filming). We put it in a nice logical order, and then she jumped all over the place. The teleprompter "promoted" and I smiled. Hanna hardly ever even glanced at it.

I wasn't worried about the filming of Hanna's seminar being "out of order." I just wanted to have Hanna on tape, for all time. I wanted her teachings preserved and documented the way she taught them. I figured that God had made editing booths for a reason. I knew the work well enough to tell the technician how to piece the program together later. That's what happened, and I don't mind saying it took me hundreds of viewings to make the edit decisions for Hanna's video to come out in an easy to follow order.

The other thing that the studio director told me was to make sure that Hanna didn't wander into the audience, as they did not have the audience lighted for camera work. I just sighed. That was like telling me to make sure Hanna didn't say "Jesus." But I agreed, and Hanna wandered into the audience anyway.

The Interpreter

Another way that I tried to help others understand Hanna's work was by accompanying Hanna to many talks and seminars and acting as her interpreter for the class. This way, I got to repeat what she was saying in front of her, over and over. She could make sure I understood, over and over.

I would also repeat the questions the students would ask her because she was hard of hearing. The groups were usually so large that she just couldn't understand a question coming from the back of the room. Sometimes a person would mumble the question or give too much information. I had the task of gathering the questions and repeating the "real question" back to her in a succinct manner, using only one or two sentences.

Hanna's soft voice needed amplification when she was speaking to groups. The problem with this is that when she would wear a lapel microphone, she would frequently blow it up, so to speak. It would just pop and crack and then boom! It would stop working. I witnessed this phenomenon on numerous occasions. Her energy field just seemed too strong for that electrical field, and trouble would follow.

In addition to this, Hanna liked to wander all over the stage and around in the auditorium. She could not be counted on to take a hand-held microphone with her. Once she would see someone in the audience in need, she was off that stage. She rarely remembered to ask the person in need to come to her, preferring to minister and teach out in the audience, especially if she wanted to make a point about a certain condition that was pertinent to the topic at hand.

She would totally forget that the other people in the audience could not see what she was doing and they could not hear her without the microphone. This would cause considerable conversation among the crowd, which added to the problem of the audience not being able to hear.

As a solution for this problem, I started following her everywhere she went with the microphone. Thus, I had the great privilege of being her microphone stand on many occasions. I learned that I could not take my eyes off her for one moment, or I would bop her in the head or mouth with the mike. This gave me the opportunity to memorize her. And sometimes, I felt that I would just get lost in the essence of the sound of her voice.

I began to feel like her, to access her energy and her teachings much easier because, in my mind, I could go right back to that seminar, right back to that essence. It was as though I knew how she would answer the question that was being asked. I learned to trust this more as the years went by. I realized that many times, when I was the one answering the question, I was just remembering how she had answered that question herself.

I was understanding and memorizing the work. I was doing the work myself, helping others. I was teaching and integrating the teachings into my own life. Still, there was so much more to learn, so much to understand. Every time I was with Hanna, I learned from everything she said or did.

A Lesson in Perception

In 1994, a few years after meeting Hanna, my company, Southern Herb, which was located in Ft. Walton Beach, Florida, was going to sponsor her to do a seminar in New Orleans. Lee and I had sponsored her there a number of times, and now Southern Herb Company was going to be the sponsor.

However, I was no longer living in New Orleans. Now I was living in the panhandle of Florida where the distance was about a five-hour drive. At the time, I did not like going into the city (or even the state). When I did go there, I saw the dirt, grime, crime, and corruption.

It was time to go to the airport to pick up Hanna. LaRae and I were driving down Airline Highway, past David Drive, and "Wow," I thought. I couldn't believe how dirty and littered and depressed the area was. Ugh.

We made comments to each other, something to the effect of, "Can you believe that this is the first impression people get of New Orleans? It's disgusting." (This is not a "judgment," I justified, just an unbiased observation.)

"Look. Look around," I said in disgust to LaRae. "Everywhere you turn your head. How can people not see it?"

Big open ditches, called "canals," were littered and overgrown. Everything looked dirty and unkempt. It was very depressing. This had been my city, but not any more, thank God.

After picking up Hanna, we returned down Airline Highway and found ourselves rediscovering the roadway from an opposite perspective as well.

"Oh, oh!" Hanna began exclaiming.

"Look, look! Look at all the beautiful flowers." (They were growing in the canals.)

"Look at all the beautiful flowers! They are everywhere! Everything is so greeeeeen!" She squealed in utter delight.

Everywhere she looked, she saw beauty. While I was looking at a piece of litter blowing on the ground, she was admiring the tiny clump of wildflowers behind it.

During the entire trip from the airport to the church, she sat on the edge of her seat, with her small face pressed against the car window, delighting in all the beauty. While driving down St. Charles Avenue (a boulevard lined with many old Victorian mansions and homes, down which the streetcars still run), she kept saying, "Oh, it's fun-to-see, fun-to-see!" (We first thought she was saying, "fantasy.")

LaRae and I looked at each other. No words were necessary. Hanna was once again striking a chord. And, yes, it is "fun-to-see."

Years earlier, I had written a song. Now it had a deeper meaning. Part of the song went:

What? What is it that you see?
Do you see beauty
That I don't see?
What, what is it
That you see?
I want to see as you
I want to look through
The eyes that you look through

And that is how I felt about my Hanna. I wanted to look through the eyes that she looked through.

Southern Herb Company

My work with Hanna at seminars and industry trade shows led LaRae and me to open Southern Herb Company, which is a wholesale distributor for Kroeger Herb Products, along with a few other lines. We started out in Florida and would later expand to Wisconsin. We started out very small. Neither of us had any money. We had knowledge, heart, love of the work, and were not afraid of working hard.

LaRae took a thousand-dollar cash advance on one of her credit cards, and that's the only loan we have ever had on the business. With this money we bought a fax machine and office and shipping supplies. We had some old sawhorses in the garage of our rented home, and there was some lumber lying around to set on top. With this and a sheet of plywood lying on top of the pool table, we had shelves for our merchandise.

Tom Brown at Kroeger Herb Company extended credit terms to us for the merchandise, and that was enough to get us going. We answered calls between loads of laundry. LaRae was driving for UPS for the holiday season to make ends meet, and I would still open my T-shirt store for a few hours on the sunny days that it felt warm enough for tourists to shop. This was in November. By January we were busy enough for LaRae or me to work all day for Southern Herb, and sometimes both of us were needed.

I was often tied up in the process of closing down my ailing T-shirt store. I had fought a good battle, but surrendered in the end. I got the message. It was time for me to use my energies for work that was more needed and more of where my heart was. It was an honorable surrender.

Southern Herb Co. has grown nicely over the years. In our early years we needed a ton of assistance from outside supporters. We were well cared for by the staff at Kroeger Herb and coached along by Tom Brown, Rick Cummings, Hanna, and my brother Mike. Throughout the years, we have been fortunate to have great employees, friends, business associates, and customers who have helped us to realize our vision to carry on Hanna's work in her lifetime and beyond.

Bobbi Brooks

While helping Hanna at seminars over the years, I also taught my own seminars. Before I was totally into my own seminar teaching schedule, I decided to ask one of Hanna's students, Bobbi Brooks, whom I had met on a number of occasions at the retreat, to come and teach a class for us in Florida.

I had hosted a number of seminars and healers, including Harvey Bevier. Now I wanted someone to come who really knew Hanna's work. Of course I really wanted Hanna to come, but she had come once already that year.

I called Bobbi, and she agreed. She had been around Hanna for about twenty-five years and knew the work well. I remember hearing her talk about some of her experiences of working with sick people during one of the sessions at the retreat. I marveled at how brave she was. I was also fascinated that she had polio when she was nine. She had been completely paralyzed, but had recovered. Her walk was labored, but she didn't limp.

Bobbi had such a loving, jolly personality. She was brilliant and wise. She could read people well and seemed to instantly know when someone wasn't "coming clean" or speaking the truth. She had a way of being with a person which allowed them to put down their facade and lay their cards on the table. She was a wonderful intuitive.

We hit it off immediately. We had respect for each other's devotion to the work and commitment to helping others. She was so funny to me. She thought I was funny, too. So we decided to try traveling and teaching together, and we have done so ever since.

Bobbi has taught me many things about energy. Of the more powerful phrases that I have heard her use is when she questions, "Is that a wise use of your energy?" She doesn't say an "allowable use" or even "right use" but rather a "wise use." The use of our energy is a choice that we make with everything that we do.

Another of the most useful and intriguing lessons she taught me was to listen to the energy behind the words someone speaks to hear if they are speaking the truth. She always says, "I hear truth in that," or "I don't hear truth in that."

At first, when I would hear her making one of those statements, I didn't know what she was referring to. What was it that she was listening to "energetically" when someone was speaking? I started to pay attention. I had been used to paying attention to how the truth *felt* in my body. To me, it felt light, like a clear, free-flowing movement; whereas, a *lie* or an untruth often felt dull or even heavy in my solar plexus (a knot in my stomach).

Different people feel truth in different ways. When I hear a profound truth, the hair stands up on the back of my neck. Some people get goose bumps or feel a light spinning sensation, all of which seem to be divine confirmation of the truth.

To listen to the sound of truth, I discovered, was to listen for a resonance, a vibrating quality. When something is said that is not the truth (whether the speaker is aware of it or not), the tone is *flat*.

This ability to "hear the truth," to discern when someone is being truthful, is a handy skill and very useful to one on the spiritual path.

Accessing Someone's Energy Field, Long Distance

Over the years, many thousands of people called Hanna for help with problems and sicknesses from which they or their loved ones were suffering. Being the extraordinary intuitive that she was, Hanna was able to tune into their energy field over the telephone and then tell them what she thought was going on.

When she would throw out the name of an herb or herbal combination that she thought would help them, it would often be the caller's first exposure to holistic health or to an herbalist, much less an intuitive healer.

She usually told the person to put their left hand on the receiver of the phone. Sometimes she used her pendulum, sometimes she would put the receiver of the phone to her third eye center, and other times she would just look toward the heavens and ask Jesus to just tell her what the problem was and what to do.

She was amazingly accurate with this. And there have been many accounts of her being able to detect something long before it would show up in a medical diagnosis. And this is what she taught her students to do.

I came to realize that what she was doing, in part, was listening to the resonance of the energy field. Sometimes I would call her about a family member's condition and she would tell me to put their hand or photo on the phone's receiver. Whenever I didn't have one of those two things available, she would tell me just to think about them. Thinking about the person brought in their energy, and then she could access their field for the help we were seeking.

Permission

Hanna always made it a point to teach us about having permission to work on someone. She said that we had karmic permission to work on someone (without having to get their verbal permission) if we were married to them or had a blood relationship to them. Otherwise, she said, we needed to ask their permission. She made it a point to say that if you run around healing people without their permission, you are violating their free will and taking the lesson on that they were supposed to learn from their condition.

Dr. Hulda Clark

With Hanna's work, we always got to hear inspirational stories of healing. Then, Dr. Hulda Clark came on the scene with some of the most brilliant work of our time. She was using an herbal program for cancer that was based on Hanna's work. The basis for her program was that parasites are always involved in cancer, as Hanna had insisted for years. She maintained that environmental toxins were the culprits for setting up an attractive environment for parasites to live. This was something Hanna had taught us too.

In her book, Dr. Clark pictured a bottle of Hanna's Wormwood combination along with clove capsules and black walnut tincture for her cancer program.

We started to hear the most incredible success stories from people recovering from a bout with cancer. We also started selling a ton of Wormwood combination. As the sales for Wormwood, cloves, and black walnut tincture went up, so did our confidence in the help that was available to people through Hanna's and now Hulda's work.

It's easy to be confident though when you don't know the people with cancer. When the disease gets close to home, your faith gets tested, as mine did.

Maureen's Breast Cancer

My sisters, Dottie and Camille, were working with LaRae and me at Southern Herb in Florida. One fateful day, we got the call I always dreaded. Someone in my family had cancer. It was our sister, Maureen, and she was scheduled for a mastectomy in three days. Previously, she had a biopsy and the doctor thought he had gotten all of the cancer, but when Maureen went back for her checkup, the prognosis was grim. The fear was that the cancer had spread and may even be in the bone marrow.

I looked at my two sisters, Dottie and Camille. None of us were crying. We were telepathically communicating, and we were focused. Our family back home in New Orleans was hysterical. The three of us each had a calm about us. I took notice of this and that is when I truly realized how much faith we all had in the work of which we were privileged to be a part. We went into action, not into fear.

Hanna had some other remedies that she thought a person should take in addition to the parasite program. We didn't want to take any chances. We had such a short period of time to work. We took all the different remedies and headed to New Orleans.

We had only three days before her surgery. She was supposed to have a radical mastectomy and the lymph glands under her left arm removed. The real concern, however, was that the cancer had spread to her bone marrow.

We all met in the living room of my mother's house. We did the five-step healing technique that Hanna had taught us for breast lump drainage. Then we did the spiritual clearing. We prayed over her, and we did a hands-on healing using the power of the spoken word. Anything we knew about trying, we tried.

Then, Maureen went home and took action. She took all of her herbs and she followed the instructions in Dr. Clark's book, *The Cure for All Cancers,* which included getting the toxins out of the environment. She had some devoted friends who helped her do all of this because it can be overwhelming to make all of these changes as quickly as they need to be made when someone is in a critical time frame.

I was just hoping to save her lymph glands. I knew this was possible, even with just three days to work. Then, a beautiful thing happened. Maureen got a chest cold. They won't operate on you when you have a chest cold, so the operation was delayed for another six days.

By the day of the scheduled surgery, Maureen was on the herbal program for nine days. When she went in for her surgery, there was not even a trace of active cancer. Surgeons removed the breast damaged by the cancer, but the cancer itself was no longer alive. As of 2004, it has been ten years now, and all is clear.

What cured Maureen? Was it prayer, was it action, was it herbs or the hands-on techniques? Who cares? All healing comes from God, anyway.

Honoring the Path One Chooses to Walk

Even with all the successes we were hearing about and experiencing, I had to learn a very difficult lesson, which is that this path is not for everyone. Sometimes it is so difficult when you know you could help someone, but he or she doesn't choose to be helped in this way. The most difficult lessons for me to learn in this field have been that everyone has the right to choose the modality for their health concerns and that it is really none of my business to impose my beliefs on them.

My friends and my family know what I do. If they want my help, they will ask; otherwise, I am to mind my own business. Always, I am called to honor the choices that they make. I am not God, and if they choose another route, even if it doesn't seem as effective to me, I am to respect that choice. I realize that we all have lessons to learn from the choices that we make and apparently, if they choose another path, they have lessons to learn from going down that path.

Each person's life is a journey of his or her soul. Some of us need to learn our lessons by getting healed, and some of us need to learn by being sick. Some need to go the medical route, and some need the eye opening awareness that often comes with alternative treatments. Hanna looked forward to the time when the two sides would work together. I am delighted to say that I see evidence of this everywhere. There are so many good-hearted people on both sides. The time is now. How fortunate we are to live at such a wonderful time in history!

Chapter 13

Vibration

Since I had always been intrigued with the mystical, the quest to understand energy went hand in hand. Understanding energy was vital to my soul, my spirit, and to my purpose in life. I realized this through my relationship with Hanna and subsequently through a few other extraordinary teachers.

My awareness had expanded to include an understanding of the reality of angels, auras, chakras, nature spirits, Ascended Masters, holy beings, gurus, and saints. I had come into a very personal relationship with the Divine and had developed a precious and intimate relationship in my heart with Jesus.

I was able to come to this place of reverence, respect, and adoration for God and the beings of the light in my own timing and through my own understanding and process. I was not forced into acceptance through fear, guilt, or pressure to "believe the RIGHT WAY." My beloved teachers had given me this gift, each one contributing in his or her own way. I was learning, in sometimes mysterious and challenging ways, that everything is energy and that the Ultimate of all energies is Love. I learned that love is the path, the expression, and the reason.

Hanna usually didn't usually refer to "energy"; she referred to "vibration." After a few years, I realized that when Bobbi and Gilda were talking about energy and Hanna was speaking about vibration, they were actually talking about the same thing.

So, I put those concepts together for consideration and contemplation.

- ✧ Everything is energy.
- ✧ Everything vibrates at its own unique frequency.
- ✧ The aura is an energy field. All things, including people and plants, have auras—so everyone and everything vibrates at a certain rate.
- ✧ God is the Ultimate of all energies.
- ✧ We share a common spirit, a oneness, which is affected when our vibration increases or decreases.
- ✧ Some things vibrate higher than others. (The more refined energies have a corresponding amount of more Light.)
- ✧ Some things vibrate at a lower or denser rate and would consequently be slower or heavier (and have less light).

Oh, I got it! I finally realized that I was now comprehending how this fit together!

The Auric Energy Field

I remember waking up one morning right after I had met Hanna for the first time, and I could see an aura around my ceiling fan. I called Belva.

"Belva, my fan has an aura," I said.

"All things have auras," Belva said.

"Even things that don't breathe?" I questioned.

"Yes," Belva said. "Everything has an aura."

Since then, I have seen many auras, mostly around people. I have no real control over when I see them, and I haven't spent too much time in that pursuit. Hanna told me not to get too caught up in trying to read the aura because she said that most of us don't know if we are looking at the aura of the physical, emotional, mental, or spiritual body. So the information won't necessarily be as accurate as we would like.

She taught us, instead, to read the energy fields of the physical body using a dowsing device. She said that most people would first be looking for help with their physical body. Most didn't even realize they might have issues in the spiritual body, much less the mental or emotional one, so concentrate on the physical.

She taught us that people seemed to "open up" spiritually as their physical body began to heal.

Viewing Energy As an "Above the Line" or "Below the Line" Concept

One day after teaching a class, I sat down and looked at a diagram I had drawn while I was teaching the section on energy. I had drawn a horizontal line, above which I had written examples of things that I knew that were high vibration (or "above the line"). Below that horizontal line, I had written examples of emotions and actions that were low vibration (or "below the line").

It looked amazing simple—easy to visualize where we were making our energetic errors, once we understood certain rules about energy.

Examples of things that are *above the line:*

Balance	Joy
Being with your	Keeping your word
family (if you get	Laughter
along)	Meditation
Compassion	Music
Discernment	Nature
Exercise	Nutritious food
Financial health	Orderliness
Flowers	Peace
Forgiveness	Playing with your child
Friendship	Prayer
Good company	Pure water
Good deeds	Respect
Good friends	Rest
Good health	Right action
Healthy relationships	Right speech
Honor	Right thought
Integrity	Seeing "God" in each other

Singing/chanting
Unconditional love
Understanding
A walk or picnic
Wisdom

Saints and holy people
Angels
The Light
Love
God!

Examples of things that are *below the line:*

Acting like you are "more spiritual" than others
Acting like you are superior to others
Addictions
Anger
Being unaccountable
Being unreliable
Bigotry
Cheating
Critical judgment
Dead/Chemicalized food and drink
Deceit
Despair
Disharmony
Dishonesty
Dishonor
Disorder
Drama queens

Egotism
Energy vampires
Envy
Faultfinding mentality
Gossip
Greed
Guilt
Hatred
Hurtful thoughts
Improper speech
Jealousy
Keeping poor company
Lies
"Out of integrity"
Pretense
Too much pride
Unforgiveness
Unkind words
Violence
Demons and dark forces

This is very simplistic, and the list is not meant "literally," as in supporting "polarity" consciousness, but rather as a way for us to see where we are making our energetic mistakes. It is intended for us to see that it is our perception, focus, attention, action, and attraction that has us experience our lives in the light of love or in the darkness of disharmonious life.

Eventually we will all come into the higher understanding of love.

Understanding Energy

Remembering that all of the things in this diagram are all part of the same whole, we draw the line so that we can understand the distinctions in our perception.

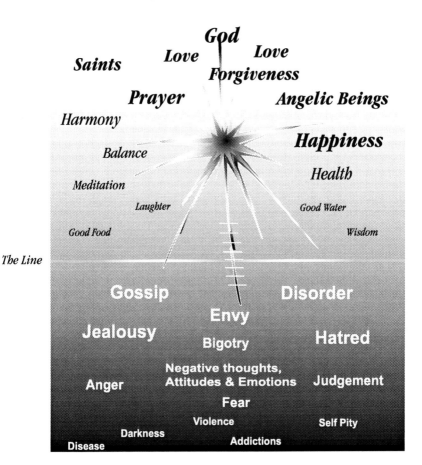

Then, as if taking dictation, I wrote the following rules of understanding energy, as I had come to understand it over the years. It went like this:

Everything is "energy" vibrating at its own unique frequency. God is the source of and the Ultimate of All Energies.

The object of the "energy game" is to stay "above the line" as much as possible every day.

The rules of the energy game:

1. Like energy begets like energy.
2. Doing things below the line pulls you below the line.
3. There is no such thing as "hovering." One is either moving up or down the scale (vibrationally) with each thought, activity, attitude, emotion, and so on..
4. Things above the line have the power to take you above the line when you've fallen below the line.
5. Things below the line do not have the power to take you above the line—no matter how unfair that seems.
6. You cannot cheat in this energy game.
7. No one else is responsible for your falling below the line; however, others do influence (sometimes greatly) our ability to stay above the line. Therefore, we must be very careful of the company we keep.
8. It's easier to stay above the line when we surround ourselves with others who spend most of their time above the line.
9. True happiness exists above the line.
10. People who spend a lot of time below the line do not necessarily want to live above the line. If they thrive on dark (upset) energy, it is necessary for them to stay there to get their energy.
11. It is not your job to get others out of darkness (or above the line). You have enough work to do keeping yourself above the line. (This does not mean that we aren't to help others, but first we must help ourselves. True service will naturally come from us when we live in the loving state above the line.)
12. A teeny-tiny bit of light eradicates darkness.
13. You will fall below the line. Do not panic and judge yourself, as your self criticism only gets you more time below the line. Acknowledge where you are and do something above the line to get you back there, fast.
14. After continued practice and perseverance at staying above the line, it does get easier at staying above the line.
15. For those traveling the "Path of Enlightenment," time below the line seems inevitable. This time helps us understand the suffering and trials of others and helps us develop needed compassion, empathy, and understanding. So, from that perspective, time at any place in the game is valuable.
16. Add your own rules as your understanding increases.

This Wasn't How Hanna Taught Us about Energy

It was not how Hanna had taught us about energy, but it was the general concept of what she taught. It had taken me ten years to understand what she and others meant when they talked about energy. Now I had found a way to make it simpler for the class so that it would not have to take them ten years.

I have heard of grade school teachers, corporate officers, nuns, ministers, and counselors using this diagram of energy as an "above the line/ below the line" concept, changing the examples to fit the people and situations because the rules of working with any energy system remain the same.

After years of referring to the energy diagram when teaching or explaining energy, I finally figured out what "the line" is. I think the line represents the ego. Everything below the line is in the jurisdiction of the ego. Things "above the line" are the jurisdiction of the heart. Free will is the key.

So, we have a choice. Who's in control? Who is directing our free will? Is it the ego in cahoots with the mind or the higher self in concert with the heart? The choice is always our own.

Negative Influences

If you have a friend who always tells you the drama and upset of their lives (or everyone else's) and you notice that after they talk to you, you feel so drained, then what?

When this happens, your life force is getting drained. If your friend is a commitment to drama and negativity, it doesn't mean you have to be.

Many times, the person doesn't even realize that he or she is so energetically draining. If you take a stand and stop allowing that energy drain, it might actually help your friend stop such an unattractive behavior.

When We Are the Ones Affecting Them

I think it is wise for us to be able to discern when it is our energy that affects another. Perhaps we are going through a tough time, and our friend just doesn't have the energy to deal with us in the way they usually befriend us. In these times, it is merciful to recognize when sharing our pain or the details of our lives is draining to them.

Sometimes Being Around Another Brings Up Our Negative Emotions

If we are uncomfortable with another human being, it's important that we not leap to the conclusion that it is the other person who brings all the negative energy into the relationship. We must not let ourselves off that easy. All of us are capable of bringing negative energy to another human being, so the presence of negative emotions in a relationship should not let anyone leap to the conclusion, "It's him (or her), not me." Others sometimes act as a mirror for us, and what we may recognize in another as intolerable behavior may well be something we know about ourselves that we find intolerable. We see evidence of ourselves, though not necessarily consciously, in their behavior or personality. In these times, it can be extremely beneficial to "stand in the fire" recognizing where this flaw or weakness exists in our own character. Learn the lesson, and be done with it once and for all.

Emotions

Emotions can be such a beautiful expression of our being. Our emotional side is to be honored, respected, and experienced.

We experience some emotions as "above the line" because they are uplifting. We experience other emotions as "below the line." These we refer to as "negative emotions."

Anger itself is not necessarily negative or below the line. The holding on to and replaying the anger is what is negative and draining.

The goal is balance. We need to walk more in the "middle of the road," because when our emotions are allowed to jerk us around, we lose our emotional balance and energy. We can enjoy our emotional nature by having control over our emotions instead of our emotions having control over us.

Don't Let My Driving Cost You Your Energy

Recently, I was driving into a shopping center which I was unfamiliar with. I was at a place in the road where I had stopped at a stop sign. I proceeded on my way pulling out into the road when a woman driving toward me from the opposite direction actually had the right of way. She was traveling all of about ten miles an hour and my pulling out ahead of her cost her about a one-second delay. There was no threat of danger or accident, just a terrible inconvenient delay of a second.

The driver had gotten so angry with me and she yelled out at me behind a scarlet red face. She had a car full of teenagers. I could lip read the words she yelled at me. They had the potential to pierce and subsequently drain my energy field had I not recognized the energy lashing out at me. I was able to purposely deflect it with my intention and laughter. I was not going to allow her anger to get stuck with me. It was her stuff, not mine. She was angry; I did not have to wear that anger.

Again, I was in amazement at how we blame others for why our lives don't work when we can't even drive in a parking lot without falling below the line.

Friendship

True friendship helps us maintain our emotional balance. What a gift it is to have a person to whom you can say anything, express any upset or emotion and who can just be a sounding board for us, without getting into our drama and upset.

It takes real skill for them to hear our "stuff" and not have it negatively affect them. This helps us to have a safe space to communicate an upset or concern. By the listener actually "hearing" what we say, we are sometimes more able to see the lesson, let the upset go and "lighten up."

For most of us it works very well to "talk things out" if we have a committed listener. At some point, we must also learn when it is wiser and more merciful to keep our own counsel.

It is useless to blame others for our experience of life. It is our life, and we are each responsible. Our state of mind and state of the heart will draw things to us to be dealt with, looked at, loved, accepted, or forgiven. But ultimately, it is our lesson. It is what we are attracting for the lessons we need to learn.

We must see why these things are "showing up" in our lives, and it is seldom "the other person," the "bad situation," or the "bogey man." Something in us attracted this energy, this lesson. What is it? What are we to learn?

Joy

Lisa Kroeger made a statement to my sister Dottie at the end of one of our summer sessions that struck me deeply. She said, **"If you don't enjoy your life, you haven't accomplished anything."**

This statement resonated in my entire body. It was like I had found a piece of the energetic puzzle I was missing! While working on myself, was I enjoying life itself? Is enjoyment a part of experiencing God in all things? *Enjoyment* is such a beautiful word — "*In* joy."

Although there are many things seemingly beyond our control which can affect our health, state of mind, and happiness, it is our duty to do the best we can to be happy, to live "above the line," to be kind and loving. We really must do our best to take the time to *enjoy* this journey.

We must learn to go through the lessons of life and to recognize those things that steal our life force and heart without judging these things or others or ourselves. And, we have to have more fun! We have a right and a duty to enjoy life, to share joy and the precious particles of energy that are created when we share goodness and good times with others. We also create these particles of energy when we do things that bring us joy, such as playing the piano or working in the flower bed or writing a letter to a loved one. In the presence of joy we feel love. Joy is the energy of the Creator, the play of the creative force. Being in the presence of the energy of joy is what it means to "be in the light."

Focus on the Light

One of Bobbi Brooks' favorite sayings is, "Focus on the light, focus on the light!" I guess that's the best advice of all. Focus on the Light. When we have our attention on the light and the things of the light, we stay centered in our heart center.

At times, focusing on the things of the light just comes naturally, but at other times it may be helpful to recall deliberately where to place our attention and focus. At times it is painful to be a human being, to go through the lessons the soul must experience, to be purified. Sometimes we lose our way, our love, and our compassion. The thing that will bring us back, time and again, is to turn our attention to the things for which we are grateful. This includes the people we love and the blessings that fill our life—in other words, to focus on the light of the One Spirit in all of us and of this magnificent creation.

Let us remember, judgment is the ultimate drain of energy, forgiveness is the ultimate mover of blockages, and to be joyful is to experience the love of God.

Forgiveness

Forgiveness is an incredibly beautiful state. Never has there been a better tool to move stuck energy than forgiveness. Forgiveness is not something a person earns; it is a place in the heart. Sometimes it is so difficult to forgive because we don't know how to do it. The beneficiary of forgiveness is the one who forgives, not just the forgiven. Please forgive. Say the words out loud, if it helps. Write letters, explain, or apologize. Do what you must, but clear the path to the heart, forgive, and ask to be forgiven.

Enjoy the grace that comes with this amazing process.

Chapter 14
Awareness of What Drains Our Energy Field

The ability to recognize negative energies, situations, people, and emotions, without judging them, requires a degree of mastery in and of itself. The ability to recognize beauty and see God in all things surely is mastery, a mastery that can be attained by each of us in this lifetime, through diligence and a loving heart.

Thoughts Are Energy

It has been proven, scientifically, that thoughts have mass. They have weight; therefore, they affect the other energy and vibrations they come into contact with.

We often bump around in our lives pretending that our thoughts are our own private property and that they don't make a difference. We maintain that we have the right to think anything we want to think and that it's nobody else's business. For the longest time, I remember thinking, "At least my thoughts are my own."

That may be true, but it doesn't mean that they are harmless.

We do have the right and free will to think whatever we want to think and let our thoughts go wherever we want them to go. But are our thoughts bringing us the happiness and peace of mind that we say we want? And, are we really directing the thoughts of the mind, or is our mind thinking whatever thoughts it wants to think? Who is responsible for the thoughts our mind thinks? What "company are we keeping" in our minds? Have we allowed our minds to become undisciplined and reckless?

Jesus said, "As a man thinketh." So, we can direct our lives with proper thinking. Yet much personal strength and discipline is required to keep our minds thinking thoughts that will direct the energy of our lives in a positive way ("above the line").

Many of us never stop to consider that we don't have to let our mind think whatever it wants. We do have a choice. When we catch ourselves thinking something negative, disempowering, or unkind, we can just say to our mind, "Thank you for sharing. Now be quiet!" Whenever the mind is under the control of the ego it is going to chatter a lot and give you all kinds of advice, judgments, and opinions. The choice to purify and direct the mind requires discipline. Some of us are even afraid of the word discipline.

Discipline Is Not a Dirty Word

Many of us have a negative feeling toward the word "discipline." We conjure up images of an authority figure asserting control over us, so we run from it. Discipline can be our friend; it can make our lives so much easier. It is required for our mental, physical, emotional, and spiritual lives to be in balance.

As we get the mind disciplined, it will be a willing follower and supporter of the purified heart—the heart as the master, the mind as a disciple.

We cannot let our minds use up our energy and misdirect our life force by being unruly, undisciplined or cruel. No matter how we justify condemning, judgmental thoughts, they will never bring happiness and peace to us or to others.

Critical Judgment

Jesus said, "To the extent that you did it to one of these brothers of Mine, even the least of them, you did it to Me." (Matt. 25:40)

We all know that we are not to judge others yet why is "judgment" such a hard thing to stop? Perhaps, because it has become entertainment. We don't even realize we are doing it. Thought by thought, word by word, many of us have a tendency to categorize and judge everyone and everything. "That's good, that's bad. He's right, she's wrong. They don't eat right. She's not a good parent. They spend too much money. He is too materialistic. She is too loud. They are too snobby. She is not spiritual enough. They don't believe the right way." On and on it goes.

On that note, let's spend a moment on the most rationalized of all judgments—bigotry (or prejudice as most people refer to it). There is so much agreement in the world that certain groups of people are a "certain way" and for that reason even God doesn't love or accept them, so we don't have to either.

Remember rule # 5: Participating in things below the line will not get you above the line, no matter how unfair that seems.

When we perpetuate bigotry, we pay the price energetically. If you hate or judge a group of people such as African-Americans, Caucasians, biracial couples and children, Jewish people, Catholics, non-Catholics, Italians, police, gay people, you are the one who pays the price by the effect that this judgment has on your life force.

Whatever we hate or hold in critical judgment, whatever we hold in disdain (whether it is in our thoughts, words or actions), we will pay the price, energetically. There is no escaping this consequence because as rule # 6 states, You cannot cheat in this energy game.

We are bound at the level of our own judgments.

Hatred is a powerful negative "below the line" force. It is so negative it should have horns. It will never get you above the line no matter how justified you think you are to feel it. I would like to see us all get the word hate out of our vocabulary altogether. Even the sound of that word is draining.

The head deceives the heart in this regard and tells the heart that it is okay to hate and judge but the heart really does know better.

Bigotry and Prejudice

The most insidious thing about bigotry is that it is a learned prejudice. Rarely is it one that we develop from our own experience. Someone shared their prejudice with us, and we allowed it to close our heart. Then we let the head justify with ridiculous explanations.

I was so fortunate to have had two parents who were not prejudiced human beings.

One of my earliest childhood memories was being a four-year-old child running down the street chasing the garbage truck and calling out the words that some of the other neighbor kids were saying to the garbage collector, "Nigger!" I said it over and over again. I saw the look on that man's face. I was a pint sized little being who was able to cripple this tall, slender man with a single word. I had hurt him, and I saw it and although that didn't feel good, I had an instantaneous experience of power. Look what I could do!

At this time, it was the late 1950s, and segregation was still going strong. This innocent man didn't challenge me; he seemed to run from me with furry. I was struck by the power of this word. My victory only lasted a few moments. Suddenly I was lifted by another upset man, my father. He carried me in his arms quickly toward our house. I could tell that I was in trouble.

The next thing I knew, my little feet were dangling above the bathroom sink, and my father was washing my mouth out with a big white bar of Ivory soap. "You had a filthy word come out of your mouth, little girl," Daddy said.

"We're going to clean that mouth out, and you will never let that word come out of this mouth again."

I was crying and crying.

"Don't you ever speak to another person that way."

I was embarrassed and I was sorry, but I was also gagging. He kept washing. I got the message. My parents were not going to tolerate treating any human being poorly, ever. My little friends had steered me in the wrong direction. I was sorry. I meant it.

My parents never pointed out any differences between people and never even talked about black people in anything but a favorable light. My little episode would be forgiven and forgotten by everyone but me. I knew that I should never be mean to others and say nasty words, but it still hadn't totally sunk in that there was supposedly something different about black people.

116

Ours was a large Catholic family raised in the suburbs of New Orleans, in a town where no black people lived. Once a black family moved into our neighborhood, and some of us kids went over to their house and played with the children. Then, they moved out within a few weeks. We were sad and didn't understand why. I thought this was by their choice. It was only as an adult that I realized that they were run out of our town. Blacks could work for us, but they could not live among us. I found out this truth when I was an adult.

On another occasion during my childhood, our washing machine had broken, and we had to go to the Laundromat. The sign above the door read, "whites only." I was just learning to read, and I read the sign slowly and out loud. I looked into my mother's laundry pile and saw a heap of colored clothing and wondered what she was planning to do now, given that the sign said, "whites only." When I questioned her about it, I could tell that it was painful for her to tell me the truth about what the sign meant.

When I was a little older, perhaps eight years old, my sisters and I would ride the bus to town. We would often sit in the back of the bus. It wasn't until I was in high school that I learned that the black people had to sit in the back of the bus. I always thought that there must be something better about the back of the bus since that's where the majority of the people were.

Another time, my mother had taken me to an appointment at the Eye, Ear, Nose and Throat Hospital. It was a hot summer day in New Orleans and the wait was long. There was no air conditioning. I was hot and incredibly thirsty. I went repeatedly to the water fountains. One time the other line was much shorter so I jumped into it. Leaning over in anticipation of a refreshing drink, I took a big slurp. My reaction was spontaneous. I spit the water out; it was as warm as sweat. I was startled. I looked over at the fountain from which I had previously been drinking, and then I looked at the sign above it, "Whites only." Next, I turned around and looked at all the people in the line behind me. They were all black. I wanted to cry. I wanted to tell them I was sorry. I wanted to let them come over and have some of my cool water from the other water fountain, but instead I just sat down and thought about how mean people can be. I had learned that lesson. Now I felt embarrassed and ashamed.

The day Dr. Martin Luther King Jr. was assassinated, my father groaned in anguish. I asked Daddy who the man was that got killed, and Daddy said, "He was a great black man who was doing a lot of good, and now someone had killed him."

Daddy squirmed and seemed uncomfortable in his body. He grumbled some other things and, although I didn't know Dr. King, I was sad too, with Daddy.

By the time I got to high school it was 1969, and segregation was over. One of my first friends was Diane Brady, a comical black girl with an infectious smile. We'd laugh and write notes, and call each other on the phone. One day after my father answered the phone and handed it over to me. I looked at him, and I realized that he was actually delighted and relieved that Diane and I were friends.

Just as bigotry and prejudice can be learned, so can tolerance, acceptance, respect, and honor. My parents taught me this by their example. What a gift they had given me!

Who Is the Boss, the Heart or the Head?

On the spiritual path we arrive at a place where we have to come into a better understanding of what is the true *navigator* of our lives. Is it our *heart* or our *head*? We have to be responsible for coming into a clear understanding with this because others will add their prejudices and their opinions, and following them can get us really lost. We have heard "follow your heart," and we have heard that we have to "listen to your head." Which one is right? Which one leads us to be the person we aspire to be?

The head is necessary and the heart is vital, so which one should guide us through the realities of human life?

When I was in college, my friend Chris and I spent most of our free time playing guitar and writing songs. One song that I wrote for Chris indicated that she must ultimately follow her head rather than her heart.

The song went like this:
I hear myself telling you
to use your head
and then I can't believe
the words that I have said
I can't believe it's me
telling you
that following your heart will never do.
But in the end, you must listen to your head (and the song went
on).

My justification was that when you follow your heart you are going to get it broken, so don't take that chance.

I really grappled with this one. I finally determined, after much consideration and contemplation, that the head must be the boss of the heart because the heart would make us too stupid, and it would have us do things that were not, ultimately, good for us. I guess I was confusing love and the power of love for something else.

It was around this time that I realized that between the two of us (Chris and me), we didn't have enough life experiences to be able to write anything of value. We would just have to finish growing up and experience life, and then maybe we would have something worthwhile to sing about.

I abandoned my dream of a song writing career, but Chris did go on to play music professionally for some years.

The Head Wants to Be the Boss of the Heart

The head sure can cause quite a racket, and it distracts us from our true nature when it is under the command of the ego. But this control is truly the divine right, duty, and privilege of the purified heart.

Each person must find what will stop all the mind chatter so that the voice of God can be heard. Different religious and spiritual traditions have in place a technique to aid in this. Catholics pray the Rosary, Native American Indians drum and participate in sweat lodges and dances, and Eastern traditions have brought us mantra repetition and the practice of meditation. Most all traditions either chant or sing. Besides being devotional, all of these help us to quiet the mind and open the heart.

Words Are Energy

Our words follow our thoughts, and our lives "show up" the way we speak them. It isn't a mystery. Our words can heal or destroy. We have power in our words. How will we use this power?

We must pay attention to what comes out of our mouths. Are our words loving? Are they empowering? Are they the truth or are they all fluffy and fake, and possibly politically correct but insincere? Do we avoid speaking the truth because we are afraid of confrontation? Do we run away from speaking the truth because we think people won't like us?

Have we misused the power of the spoken word? If we want power in our spoken word we have to respect the words that come out of our mouths. To respect our own words, we must speak the truth. Sometimes this is not easy especially when we have to deliver a communication that might be upsetting or painful to another. At these times we must be especially clear about our intention. What do we intend to accomplish with the delivery of this communication? When your intention is clear, then ultimately even a painful communication will be the kindest thing.

Werner Erhard said, "People can hear the truth, but lies make people crazy."

The road to the heart is through truth, kindness, forgiveness, and love. Sometimes the kindest action is not always perceived as being loving. But how can we travel this road to the heart when we are afraid to speak our own truth for fear of offending someone or meeting with disapproval? Speak your truth with the intention of communicating the real issue. If you offend someone, then clean it up as best as you can but do not let this stop you from being truthful. Also, let us not use the truth to dump on people. Sometimes things just don't need to be said. This is when discernment is necessary.

Watching the words that come out of our mouths doesn't mean we can't be funny or silly or tell jokes. But when you become a better communicator and are clear about where you are coming from with your communication and your motivation and intention are clear, then you will probably notice that your jokes are actually funnier because you are coming from a different place. Many people use joking as a way to communicate something that they are unwilling or unable to communicate otherwise. Many a truth is said in jest. But when the intention is pure and from a place of lighthearted goodness, laughter follows and everyone feels uplifted.

Objects Hold and Emit Energy

Objects also hold energy. They can become impregnated with energy, and they have their own energy field which they emit. Hanna loved objects that could be used as healing tools or "gadgets," as she affectionately called them. She gave us a number of them to work with when we needed to move certain kinds of energy.

She used her soma board for detoxifying additives and preservatives from food and from our bodies. This little board does not suck the preservatives out but rather neutralizes most of them on an energy level. She designed another board called the pico board for food that had been irradiated; a water revitalizer for restoring the magnetic integrity to water; a bio-energy disk for the lymphatic system and for adverse effects of scanners. She had us use a computer pillow for those of us who spend a great deal of time in front of the computer and are thereby exposed to that radiation. Hanna was always coming up with gadgets, and the more we used them, the more uses we found for them.

Through gadget work and lessons with Hanna, Bobbi, Gilda and others, I came to understand how objects in our environment can affect us. Haven't you ever picked up an object, and put it right down? Something repelled you from it, and you didn't even know what. Objects hold and emit energy. Have you found yourself unconsciously petting or stroking some object only later to find out that it belonged to some warm, loving person?

The Necklace

I have a friend who is a Native American Indian. His name is Milo Beaver. Milo and I met Hanna on the same day at that first New Orleans seminar. Milo was one of Hanna's favorite Native American Indians. Milo is still in touch with his heritage and consequently has the gift of seeing energy fields. Hanna said that American Indians are born with the gift of seeing, and she was actually taught to "see" the beings of other dimensions by a little Indian girl who was living with her.

At one of Hanna's seminars, he told a friend of mine, (whom he had just met), that he would advise her to stop wearing the necklace she had on because it was obviously given to her by someone who was quite angry with her. There was angry energy vibrating and irritating around her neck.

I knew the giver of the necklace, and I knew that Milo was right on! My little friend took that piece of jewelry off right away, even though she had loved it. She admitted that she had felt strange when wearing it. But she loved the man who had given it to her and had hoped that someday he would love her back again.

We need to listen to those instincts. When we pick up on some message that we don't want to hear, we turn away and hope that we are wrong. We need to stop and listen.

This brings us to a good reason for keeping holy articles around whether we wear them or have them in our home. The energy field penetrates our energy field to uplift us and bless us.

Possessions Hold Your Energetic Imprint

I am aware that certain energy fields are not conducive to my own; therefore, I do not usually lend out my clothing or borrow clothing from others. In many cases, I would rather not sleep on someone else's bed because I am sensitive to their energy fields and I can feel their thoughts and emotions. This is why it's a good idea to know how to clear energy fields. I travel so frequently that I have to be able to sleep in a bed at the hotel.

There are many ways to clear energy fields and devices you can use, and I would advise reading some of Hanna's work for techniques. For now, let's remember the technique we have that is always available to us—prayer. A sincere prayer from the heart with a blessing and a command for all those energies to leave is easy to do and is effective.

The People Around You Impact Your Energy Field

The people in our lives have such a tremendous impact on our energy fields that we have to be diligent about the company we keep. Many of us feel obligated to allow certain people in our lives, even though they drain us.

Remember a time when you felt really good, energized, and happy? Then, in walked your neighbor or relative with gossip or complaints. Or perhaps this person came to share the drama of his or her life or God-knows-whose life, and when he or she leaves, you feel like you could fall on the couch from exhaustion. "I'm so drained," you moan. Drained of what? Energy, real energy, physical and emotional energy. The kind of energy it takes to run your life. Can you afford that?

Energy Vampires

An *energy vampire* is one who gets his or her energy by draining us of ours. We have all been energy vampires at some point, but some people are that way most of the time.

Energy vampires need "below the line" energy to survive. They get this by being around upset, anger, drama, or pity energy. This is their fuel.

If they don't have any upset energy around them, they create it. They can get you upset or feeling sorry for them in very little time. If they can't get you upset about one topic, they'll try another, because they know where your weak spots (energy taps) are. They can "hook in" quickly.

Energy vampires do not consciously know what a negative effect they are having on others. And sometimes pointing this out to them can make them stop. Most of us really do want to be good, uplifting people. But a chronic energy vampire is usually a master manipulator of energy. They know how to "get to you." Haven't you heard yourself say, "She really got to me"?

But even though energy vampires don't realize how negative they are or how they drain us, they get energy from it. If they realize the negative effect they are having on others and want to change, they will have to make positive changes in their lives so that they will be able to source their own energy. This takes a commitment to change the behavior patterns, and sometimes that requires a considerable amount of hard work and truth telling. It's a big step, one very worth taking.

The Coffee Shop

There is a little coffee shop that I frequent. A while back, I went into this normally cozy and friendly environment to find the staff upset and the energy strained. I asked the two behind the counter how they were doing, and they apparently had been energetically drained by a customer and just didn't know what exactly happened or what to do to release the energy.

When they told me the story, I could profile the customer.

The story goes something like this. Every day this woman comes in, and every day she finds fault with something. They don't serve her fast enough, they don't have a tea (that they never had), and they don't have half-and-half milk out, only whole milk—always some terrible thing.

The employees always cringe to see her coming but until this day they were always able to grin and bear the verbal abuse she would wage against whoever was behind the counter.

I have been in this shop many times, and I have never experienced the staff to be anything but congenial. Apparently, this woman sees the same staff through different eyes. I assert that it is not only the staff at the coffee shop that she sees that way.

Anyway on this particular day, she just couldn't be satisfied. After everything was wrong with everything the staff did, she commented, "Why does it always have to be a problem here?"

One of the employees tried to soothe her, to which she hurled a few more statements of a commitment to stay discontented. When she walked out the door, she left the place "energetically slimmed." One of the employees followed her outside and politely spoke his mind, asking her not to be so ugly but to communicate her upset responsibly and to allow them to make things right.

This was not the kind of woman who wanted to be satisfied because satisfaction would blow her energy game. She is an energy manipulator or energy vampire. You can bet that wherever she goes, upset follows. She needs upset to tap into the energy field. If upset is not present, she will create it to have a negative energy field to tap into. Negative energy feeds her.

123

Once the employee called her on her racket, her cover was blown. If she can't come back and get them upset, then she can't get their energy. She has not returned—which would prove to be a great relief to the crew at the coffee shop, but meanwhile the problem is that she had messed up the energy in the shop. The employees could still feel her ugliness there for quite a while. Things did not go well the rest of the day in that shop, even when the shift changed and another group of employees came in.

Now you can probably identify at least a person or two who fits into the category of energy vampire for your life's energy. So, what can you do?

What Can We Do About Someone Who Drains Us?

Don't let energy vampires or negative people into your field. Once you no longer provide them with a place to tap in and refuel, they will leave you alone. They will feel frustrated and go away.

The problem is that you will have to be willing to let them go. That's often the real issue. For some reason, you don't want to let them go. You identify some self worth with having them around or with trying to help them. You must understand that letting them feed off you in no way helps them or you. It does not make you a better person; it makes you a more exhausted one.

Compassion

It is very often appropriate to listen to someone's hurt or upset and to be there for them at their time of hardship or sorrow. Life beacons us to be compassionate. This is a totally different use of energy than what is required to deal with someone who is a "chronic malcontent." It is not a wise use of energy to let anyone use up your life force; however, it is always wise to be compassionate.

What Can I Do If I Get Stuck with Some Negative Energy?

The left side of the human body is the receiving side. So don't listen to an angry or upset person, with the receiver of the phone up to your left ear. As soon as you realize that the caller is going to speak with anger or upsetting words, change the receiver to the right ear. Do whatever you can to avoid taking negative energy into your body. This helps tremendously if you understand what you are doing energetically.

Sometimes, before you know what's happening, you have some upset energy stuck in your body. Maybe you listened with the receiver to the left ear, or someone walked into your home or office and spoke with upsetting words. All of a sudden, you realize that this negative energy is stuck in your body because you now feel upset. What can you do? Close off your left hand and shake it out your right hand with the intention to release the unwanted energy.

If shaking your hand out is not enough, go outside to Mother Earth and find a patch of grass. Take off your shoes, and breathe through the souls of your feet imagining that you are breathing the earth up through your feet. Nice, slow, deep breaths. Take the support of Mother Earth. She loves to help us in this way and can easily clear negative energies for us. It only takes a few seconds or minutes, and the unwanted energy is gone from your body.

Of course, prayer, songs, and chants are old favorites for removing negative influences, so we always have that option.

Don't let an upset person look into your left eye. Again, your left side is your receiving side.

Don't keep letters, photos, or personal articles in your possession from someone who brings you down or chronically upsets you. This is a tap into your field, and it does nothing to uplift you.

Clearing Dark or Negative Energy Fields

Bless your house with holy water or bless some salt and throw it into the corners of the rooms. The darker, denser energies go to the corners. So blessing the corners takes care of the whole room.

Hanna taught us to say, "In the name of Jesus, get out of here, get out of here. Dark Forces (or disincarnate entities, or demonic forces), get out of this building, get out! You are not welcome here. You must go! In the name of Jesus, I command you to leave this home/ building/ room/ person. Go to the light. Go with Jesus to the light. He can help you; we cannot. Leave! In the holy name of Jesus, I command you to leave now!"

Use the power of your spoken word to claim your space for the good of yourself, your family, and your office mates.

There are many other techniques that can be used for dark force removal. The one I have used the most is the seven-candle ceremony. You can find it in Hanna Kroeger's book, *The Seven Spiritual Causes of Ill Health*.

Make sure you do your own spiritual protection before working on others. Do not give Dark Forces the option of staying with you or in this dimension.

Calling the Angels

Whenever Hanna would call on Jesus to help with these difficult cases, she would usually call on the angels first. Maybe they roll out the energetic red carpet for Him. Certainly they accompany Him wherever He goes. It always feels good to me when I call them. The act of inviting or welcoming is such a sweet gesture, and the angels rejoice when the invitation is extended.

Then you can say, "Jesus, please come and be with us as we do this work in Your name."

Then wait a few seconds. He is fast. He comes as soon as you call Him.

You may also want to remind yourself and the people with you, "Jesus said, whenever two or more of you are gathered in my name, I will be with you." I can always feel His presence when I speak those words out loud.

Then start with the words like this:

"In the name of Jesus, I command all negative entities and dark forces and darkness out of here!"

It is a powerful command. Repeat it over and over with love in your heart. You are doing a very great service for them as well as for the person to whom they have attached.

"In the holy name of Jesus, I command that you leave me (or this house or building) now!"

It's a good idea to open a window or a door when you are commanding these energies out (not that they need to go through the open door), but perhaps because it brings in some fresh energy, as the stale energies are exiting.

Dark forces don't like the smell of sage, cinnamon, eucalyptus, peppermint, or incense from holy places. They don't like the sound of sacred chants, devotional hymns, or prayers from the heart, and they really don't like a crucifix.

Sometimes these entities do try to attach to people in the light. They do this for a number of reasons, perhaps seeking the enlightenment or light of that person, or out of fear, or even because of attachments to things or people in this dimension. If you feel that a negative energy, negative entity, or a dark force has attached to you and you are unable to get a release do the following: go to a window or door and open it. In a firm and powerful voice shout "Rockma!" Repeat it as many times as you need to until you feel that all is clear.

If you feel this entity is strong and potentially dangerous, then before you command it out, call on the angels. They know what to do and will bind the dark energy and escort it away properly.

Pray. Claim your energetic space. State that this is a house of God or the Holy Spirit or the Great Spirit or whatever name you call God, and affirm that this space is only for the beings of the light and no lesser energies are allowed to penetrate your field.

Direct the Energy of Your Life

It is time for us to come forward and direct the energy of our lives by taking responsibility and by taking a stand. For what are you willing to? Taking a stand is a powerful place that calls in energy to support that stand.

Once someone asked me if I spent time each day in prayer and if I prayed a certain way. This person was sure that I was not praying and was reprimanding me in her own way. I laughed to myself as I remembered that I had turned my life over to God as a prayer, and now considered my every action and thought as a prayer. I had taken this stand and claimed that it would be so. She would have no way of knowing this nor was it any of her business, but I also realized that, in her own way, she loved me and just wanted to make sure that I was in good with God.

Fortunately, we have entered a time where the goodness of people, the importance of the Spirit in All, and the connection with each other and the One Spirit of God are being honored and are being given center stage. More media time is being spent on this kind of story than ever before. How fortunate we are to live in such a blessed time as we take part in these new and more loving energies that are now pouring into our lives!

Chapter 15

Energy Flow

Harvey Bevier is the one who gave us the information on main supply energy. Main supply is that amount of energy that is required to run that particular energy system or maintain that particular field. It is usually energetically inappropriate to give out of your main supply. We should give from our overflow.

On the topic of money, let us look at an energetic system and watch what things affect such a system.

The Energy We Call Money

Imagine your money life to be like a bike wheel with the spokes representing the energy pathways and the center of the wheel, or hubcap, being you. Each financial relationship that you have is an energetic pathway in your life. The degree to which these pathways are open and the energy is moving is the degree to which money (or finances) will work in your life.

If you pay all of your bills every month, you keep those channels open and clear. And if you are able to provide for yourself and your family and live a comfortable life, then your relationship with money works. Whether you are living off of $20,000, or $200,000, or $2,000,000 each year, your money works only to the corresponding degree that your money energy channels are open.

If you do not pay a bill, you temporarily block the energy in that pathway. Let's say you pay half of your bills each month, then half of your energetic pathways are blocked, and you can't expect to experience true financial abundance.

Energetic pathways can be blocked even if you pay all of your bills every month, but you have a friend who owes you money and neglects to pay you back. Every month she doesn't pay you, this blocks that particular channel. If, on a month that she cannot pay, you make a new agreement (let's say she agrees to give you all the money when her income tax refund check arrives), then you have kept that energy channel flowing for both parties, until such time that her check arrives. If she pays you, the channel remains open. If she doesn't pay, it's blocked again.

If there is a bill that you never pay because of some flimsy justification such as, "That company makes too much money anyway" or "Besides that lawn mower was a piece of garbage," that channel is permanently blocked, until such time as you start paying again.

Forgiving a Financial Debt

On the subject of forgiveness, if someone owes you money and you know that you are never really going to get it back, do what you have to do to forgive the debt. Then don't lend them any more money. You may be okay with this energy channel being blocked for you, but do you really want to help them block another channel for themselves? They are borrowing money from you and not paying it back. Obviously they already have other pathways blocked in their "financial energy system." Do you want to contribute to their problem by creating yet another blocked channel?

If someone owes you money, or if you owe someone money, and the original agreement for repayment is not being met, take some positive action. Work out a payment plan that the two of you can agree upon and that the debtor can really keep (like five dollars a month for the next fifty years). This will get energy moving down that vein again. It may be a slow moving vein but at least it will be moving.

So many of us don't know why money doesn't work for us. If we would sit down and draw out a diagram of our financial energetic relationships, the mystery would be over. The task at hand would be clear. Any place that there is a channel of slow moving or non-moving energy, something has to happen. A new agreement has to be made and kept or repayment has to begin.

When bankruptcy is inevitable, make sure your integrity is as clear as possible. In other words, don't go charging up your credit cards because you know you are going bankrupt. Bankruptcy is a compassionate tool provided to us so we don't have to kill ourselves when things go too far astray, financially, and we see no other way out. If we are faced with bankruptcy and surrender to the process and protection of it, we must be committed to a new relationship with money, energetically. If we don't honor and respect a fresh relationship with money and repeat the same mistakes, we will have to learn the lesson again. The next financial disaster could be much more severe with more far reaching consequences.

Energy Leaks

Often our lack of energy is not because someone is being difficult or negative or vampiring us, but because we have leaks in our own field. What causes these leaks? Incompletions, things gone unhandled or unacknowledged from the past and present create leaks. Stepping over an issue, hoping it will go away, or pretending that it doesn't exist can create leaks, as does living in the past and worrying about the future. Being "out of integrity," dishonest, non-forgiving, cheating, unloving, and all "below the line activities" leaks our precious energy. But it's not just that alone.

We lose a lot of our energy because we are truly good-hearted energy idiots. We go way past where our intuition tells us to stop.

Here's a typical example: You've worked all week and just need some time off with your family to hibernate in the sanctuary you call home. Someone calls you and asks you for help moving. You don't have the energy, but you just can't say no. So you go. Your family needs you, your house needs you, and your body needs you to rest and regain your energy. Maybe the next day you would be revitalized, and it would be appropriate then, but you go anyway. Energy leaks.

On the other hand, maybe you never go. You never offer a helping hand. You are a lazy, self-centered slug. You keep it all to yourself. Energy leaks.

If you want to be happy, be around happy people. If you want to keep a positive attitude, hang out with positive people. If you want to be productive, be around productive people. If you want a vital life force energy field, be a shepherd. Watch your flock.

Begin to identify those areas where you lose your energy.

Start to notice what is happening when you start to feel drained. Where do you feel it in your body? What are the circumstances? What is the pattern? Who or what is always present?

I have traveled extensively teaching seminars. When I am teaching, I am giving it all. I'm not holding anything back. I came to lay it out, and I do my best to do that. When I come back in town, I can't jump right back into my office scene and put on the business person hat. I can't answer any more questions about anything. I have to give it a rest. No matter how much I have tried to talk myself out of this phenomenon, it doesn't help. I have to rest and be away, at least one day and usually two. When I do go into the office on these two days, I have learned to be very gentle with myself and not expect too much. For whatever I accomplish, I give myself accolades.

I have also identified that when I come back after a week or so of travel, I am in an extremely open space and I can cry or get emotional at the silliest of things, so I have learned to sit back and let it be okay. I'm vulnerable; it's kind of sweet when I remember to make room for it. It's also kind of goofy when I find myself tearing up because the copier has run out of paper. It's time to go home and regenerate, maybe for three days.

So that's the kinds of things that I was learning over the years. Everything is energy. Everything makes a difference.

The Time Is Now

Now is the time. There is so much that we can do, think, or say to uplift the world in which we live. Let's enjoy our time together. Let's enjoy the funny, endearing, and trying things about each other. Let's remember that each of us is doing our best.

The path is love, the fuel is right action, and the ticket to bypassing the roadblocks is forgiveness. We can walk this path; each one of us can do it.

Lighten Up!

It is very useful to be able to recognize when someone or something is negative or is behaving from a lower vibrational nature. This allows us to make choices that support our well-being; however, running around avoiding the darkness in people, is not the answer, as you cannot chase the darkness away. Light absorbs the darkness. Your light and your love, compassion, and kindness can transform lives. Your seeing the "good and the light" in others is the kindest of the kind, the most loving, the most honoring of God's children, regardless of their faults and flaws.

Let us not take ourselves so seriously. Being "spiritual" doesn't have to mean being stern or serious. Lighten up. Have fun. Laugh. Enjoy the journey.

Fortunately we have so much help available to us. All we need to do is ask and be willing to listen and follow instructions.

When the student is ready, the teacher appears.

Chapter 16

The Last Season

After my "awakening," my friend Tommy thought that I could get some real support by listening to some tapes of Gurumayi. I was still so broke I couldn't afford to buy them, but that didn't matter because Tommy kept me supplied with chanting tapes, talks on tape, photos, and beautiful books with uplifting stories of holy people and spiritual messages.

I was feeling so much more peaceful in my life in general, and I adored listening to this one particular tape. It was a melodic version of a sacred mantra. The mantra was in Sanskrit, and the meaning is, "I bow to God who dwells in my own heart." I sincerely meant this, with every repetition.

Tommy told me to repeat it over and over and over again, to sing it, to say it, to think it. This action would help me to still my overactive, undisciplined mind, raise my vibration and would support me on my spiritual path.

I followed this great advice, and I repeated it even in my sleep.

Tommy said that a true guru is a teacher who, through his or her teachings, would really help you with your ego. I had made some progress with my ego but I had to admit that it was still in the driver's seat. I welcomed the support. I was now smart enough to know that I could use all the help I could get.

The Ashram

After a while, I was fortunate enough to go to Gurumayi's ashram, which is a huge spiritual community visited by people from all over the world.

The thing that touched me the most was that it felt like the holiest place that I had ever been. And that energy totally nurtured and soothed me. The presence of God was palpable.

It was a spiritual retreat, and it was obvious that the participants were there for that reason. There was such a powerful and pure energy that permeated everything. I was impressed by how much I was really able to just focus on the inner work that needed to be done. There were programs, meditation halls, dining halls, and beautiful buildings and grounds. Everything was so well cared for and respected.

I was surprised with how many different kinds of people were there. There were people from countries that I had never even heard of. There were people from every different religious and ethnic backgrounds. There were nuns and priests and rabbis and shamans. There were grandparents and babies and teenagers and young adults.

I estimated the crowds to be around 3000, yet, there was such tranquility and silence.

The mantra or some equally beautiful chant was always playing over the sound system, so it was easy to maintain a state of serenity. I loved going there, and I made it a practice to go at least once a year. It was my retreat.

I also realized that I needed all the guidance I could get from holy people, and I cherished the opportunity to be around Gurumayi, the energy of such a place, and the opportunity to get a different perspective on my spiritual life.

Dreams

Throughout the years, I was imbibing the lessons I was learning into my life. I was making changes at a rate that allowed them to be life-style changes.

I had a few very powerful dreams and shared them with some of my friends. We would share our interpretations. I wished I could dream more. My friend advised me to use Hanna's "crystal laser light" on my third eye center before I went to bed.

"But the crystal laser light is for the immune system and clearing negative energies," I said.

"I know," she said. "But it works for dreams too. Try it."

"Okay, tell me what to do," I said.

"Just hold it up to your third eye center (between the eyebrows) and hold it there for about thirty seconds. Do this right before you are ready to go to sleep. As you are holding it, ask God for dreams that will lead and guide you—and that you will understand and remember."

"Okay," I said.

What did I have to lose? I felt like a unicorn when I was holding that light to my forehead. The crystal laser light is really not a laser at all. It is an inexpensive flashlight with an attachment. The attachment has some items in it such as herbs, golden crystals, and a magenta lens with a series of Atlantean numbers on it. When the light from the flashlight shines through the attachment, it clears the darkness from the energy field and uplifts or raises the vibration of the thing at which it is pointing.

I had used this device many times for clearing negative energies from rooms or articles, but I had never thought of it for dreams or intuition.

After that, my dreams got so vivid. Some of them have actually been prophetic. I would ask for dreams to lead and guide me before I would go to sleep at night. Sometimes the messages have been so clear. Sometimes I have had no doubt that they would come true. On a number of occasions I actually went back in my dream journal and marked the day when that particular dream came to fruition.

I learned to trust them more. I learned to distinguish between a dream that I was having for therapeutic reasons, dreams that were just nonsense, and dreams that were prophecies.

I had one such dream about four or five years after meeting Gurumayi. It was about Hanna.

I Had Dreamt of Hanna's Passing

In 1995, I had this dream. It was very vivid and very real. When I awoke I knew it was important.

In the dream, Hanna and I were both at Gurumayi's ashram in the mountains. The grounds there were very beautiful, and the atmosphere was serene. I was outside in front of the main dining hall, which is a majestic building with high marble steps and huge marble columns, like an old courthouse. The scene was so vivid and fresh for me. I was soaking in the beauty of the surroundings, the rolling landscape, the trees, and the air.

The snow was beginning to fall. It was the first snowfall of the season, and the flakes were large and soft as they danced in the air and fell slowly to the ground. The first snowfall of the season is always so magical to me, so special, so purifying. The snow was falling slowly in big, beautiful flakes, and I was lifting my hands as if in an attempt to catch the flakes. I was delighting in the feeling that I was having both internally and externally. I felt such a sense of total peace. I was in bliss, enjoying the enchantment of the moment.

Then, one of the people, who had been assigned to be Hanna's attendant, came to summons me.

"Hanna wants you to come to her," she said. "She is going now."

I went to her bedside. She was lying on her bed in a sweet room that had been made very special for her. She was dying. I knew that everything was okay. She was in peace, and she was happy, and she was here, in this holy place, being well cared for.

Hanna took my hand and told me that she wanted to tell me a few more things before she went. I knelt by her side holding her hands, and she told me. The attendants were nearby, but they let us have our time. I laid my head on Hanna's chest and listened intently to her words. I loved her so completely.

When I awoke, I remembered every detail of that dream except the messages that she gave me. I know that this is no accident. I know that I will remember them when the time is right.

The thing that I did absolutely know was that Hanna's time on this earth was short, and I would have a warning when the time was close.

After the Dream

After I awoke from the dream, I thought maybe I was supposed to take Hanna to the ashram. I knew that Gurumayi knew of Hanna and her work and would welcome her. I took a few futile stabs at making this happen but clearly that was not the message of the dream, as it did not seem to be a drive that Hanna had, although she did say that she would like to meet Gurumayi.

I dropped this idea, figuring that if it was supposed to happen, it would.

I was busy with running my own business, doing the work, and teaching seminars. And I was in regular contact with Hanna concerning questions and things I needed clarification on.

The Last Seminar Season

In the beginning of 1997, Hanna had said that she was not going to travel anymore. She told me that she wanted to stay home and devote more time to writing. She needed time at her home, and each year her summer retreat schedule seemed to extend itself on both ends, so there was always much going on.

Then in mid-1997, she said that she would do a few more seminars, which means she actually only took one season off. She talked to me about her desire to travel again. I offered to travel with her and assist her. I called Tom and I found out that Hanna had talked to him about this already. Tom Brown was not happy with her desire to travel again. He thought that she was in too weakened a condition and that at eighty-four years old, she had the right to stay home.

But Tom knew Hanna well, and he knew that she was going to do it regardless of his objections. Both of us were concerned about her traveling, and neither of us thought she should go anywhere alone again.

Tom asked me to provide him with a list of the cities that I thought Hanna should go to. Then he discussed the potential travel schedule with her and had her pick a few cities. We agreed I would accompany her and help her in whatever way I could.

The cities Hanna picked were Toronto, Canada; Madison, Wisconsin; Tampa, Florida, and Atlanta, Georgia. She would also do two events in her home state of Colorado.

Hanna's Seminar in Madison, Wisconsin

We had a hard time finding a place large enough to hold Hanna's seminar. We finally were able to get the chapel at St. Benedict's Monastery. The chapel could hold 200 people. This was the first time that Hanna was going to come to Madison, and we were not sure what the turn out would be. But we did know we could get many people as she had students in all of the surrounding states.

The seminar sold out weeks in advance. We could have sold 500 tickets. Although we had ample time to prepare, nothing would prepare me for the condition that Hanna was in when she walked off the plane. I was in shock. She looked so tired and so frail. How would she do this seminar and the three that followed so closely after?

We stopped at the restroom to let her collect herself and freshen up before going into the seminar room. She took her time in the girls' room. She took a little extra time. I had to go in and check to make sure she was all right, and, sure enough, she was doing a little primping in the mirror.

On the way up to the seminar room, she stopped to help a lame person, so I knew she was getting fired up.

The Seminar Begins

Although we had rented a professional sound system and had a competent person to run it, the sound gave us trouble from the start as the room echoed fiercely. The people in the middle and the back of the room could not hear Hanna. The marble floors and the high-pitched ceiling made the sound hollow. It sounded like she was talking into a seashell. As it was, her voice was soft and her accent heavy. Now the tinny echoing sound made it impossible for some to understand her.

Hanna was not distracted—everyone else was, especially me. We had tried to be so prepared for all of this, but we didn't get the problem worked out until the next day. It didn't bother Hanna; she just saw a full house and seized the opportunity to teach and help whomever she could. I wanted things to be so perfect for Hanna and for the participants, and I was horrified that we could not get the sound right.

By the second day, the sound was working better. By the end of the seminar, we were pleased that all had gone well, and the participants had seemed pleased.

The seminars were all two-day events, Friday night and all day on Saturday. By Saturday, Hanna was back to her old self. She presented a wonderful seminar, and now it was time to take her to the airport.

One of the seminar participants came up and asked us if we had heard that the Denver airport was closed. Of course we had not heard of any such thing. We had been totally immersed in the logistics and details of the seminar. Just because the Denver airport was supposedly closed did not mean that Hanna would decide to sit still and stay in Madison another day. Oh, no, she had to get home in time to lead the church service in the morning, and they would just have to open the airport for that.

I told Hanna that I had checked and the airport was closed in Denver. Hanna told me to call her home and ask what the weather was there. I called and her sister, Beatrice, who was living with Hanna, answered the phone. She confirmed that the weather was outrageous and that, in fact, there had been a blizzard.

Hanna was still not satisfied.

"Well, all right," I remembered thinking. I knew my Hanna and I knew we were still going to the airport and away we went. It was just slightly snowing, but apparently the blizzard was moving our way. We got to the airport in Madison. It was open, but the Denver Airport was not, so Hanna could not get on an airplane. As much as I loved to spend time with Hanna, I did not like to be with her when she wanted to be going home. She was not happy.

We went back into our cozy apartment. After a little while, and a hot bowl of lentil soup, some good bread, and a fresh salad, Hanna was content to stay put and go out the next day. She went to bed early and slept through the night. She was up early the next morning. She was rested, refreshed, and ready to go.

"Hanna, I don't think the airports are open yet. I'll have to check," I said into the pouting face of a child.

Sure enough, they weren't open.

Throughout the day, the snow came down harder, and Hanna napped and ate and worked on her book at the desk in her bedroom. Periodically, I would check on her and discover that she had fallen asleep at the desk. One time, I was actually able to convince her to lie down in the bed.

Another time, she was in the room writing, and I slipped in and handed her a photo of Gurumayi. I was interested to see what she would have to say about her. She studied the photo and touched it. I decided to leave her alone, and I would ask her later. When I returned she had again fallen asleep on the desk. This time, she fell asleep on Gurumayi's photo. When she looked up from her sleepy state, she handed me the photo and said very plainly, "This one is enlightened."

When she was sufficiently rested, she came out into the kitchen and watched me prepare an early evening meal. I was totally aware of the fact that she was watching everything that I was doing in the kitchen. I was also fully aware that all the things I knew to do right in the kitchen were the result of her teachings.

I had fresh vegetables, which I washed in apple cider vinegar and/or salt water. I had whole grains and nuts and seeds to add to the fresh salad that I had chopped without a food processor (she said that they killed the vibration of the vegetables), and I had seasonings without pesticides or additives or preservatives. I used real butter and olive oil and nothing fake or over processed. She watched it all. She nodded in approval.

"Hanna," I asked, "will you help me when you go?"

"What?" she asked as if needing clarification.

"When you go. When you pass on. Will you help me with my work?"

"I will help whoever asks," she said.

"Well, I'm asking you Hanna. Will you help me?"

"Then yes, I will," she said.

I was surprised at myself for being so forthcoming, but I had to know.

As we spoke, I noticed the backdrop scene. Hanna was sitting at the counter and behind her were my sliding glass doors, through which I could see the first snowfall of the season. The flakes were large and floated slowly to the ground.

It was so beautiful. I looked at Hanna, and the ashram scene dream came back to me. Here she was, sitting with me, comforting me, telling me some things I needed to know before she left. The time was very near.

For three days and three nights, she stayed with us. When she needed to rest, she rested. When she was hungry, she ate something delicious. When she wanted to work, we left her to her work, except for the time she wanted all three of us to work on a world political problem. LaRae and I gathered up every holy or sacred object we could find and brought it to her with a map of the world so that she could do her work.

She was very fond of her "map work." She would take a map of the United States or the world or whatever area she wanted to work on and pray over it and check out the energy on different areas or states or cities and then go to work. She would put holy objects or prayers or anything that represented the energy of what she thought the region needed, like water. If there was a drought somewhere, she'd put a glass of water on that state. If there were a problem with too much rain, she would put a picture of the sun. Whatever was needed, she felt compelled to ask God for by working with energy in this way. She kept her huge map set up at all times.

Anyway, this time we weren't working on a map, we were working on a political figure from another country. She thought he was very misguided. She blessed some salt and poured it all over the photo of him from the newspaper. Then we let some holy objects stand on the article about this man and his trip to the United States.

Doing this work reminded me of the first time I ever saw Hanna use a map for energy work. It was during one of my first summer classes probably the summer of 1988. This was when I was still living in New Orleans, prior to moving to Florida. She pulled out a huge map of the United States. After showing us some map work, she told us that we could use a map to do other kinds of energy work, such as to determine where a missing person might be or to find out where we should live.

"Just ask the Lord where you should live so that you can best serve Him," she said. "Then put your pendulum over the map and find the answer," she said with confidence.

At the time I could not imagine ever living anywhere but in the South, close to my large and loving family. Hanna took my hand, and holding the pendulum and moving it over the map, it began to twirl like a helicopter. "Wisconsin!" she proclaimed boldly into my expressionless face.

At the time I didn't know that Hanna or God could read minds because I remember thinking while still smiling at my sassy, little teacher, "Wisconsin? Yeah right. Well God is just going to have to get over that one."

I had no desire even to visit Wisconsin. I knew nothing about the state except that it was in the North and it was cold there.

" God, just give me option number two. I don't want to go to Wisconsin. I am not ever going there, sorry," I said as if I had the last say.

Sitting in Wisconsin with Hanna these nine years later, I was ready to hear and to do whatever God or Hanna wanted. We took three trips to the airport during these three days. When she wanted to go, we just went. On the drive back from the airport from the second trip, she fell asleep in the back seat and curled up with a blanket. LaRae said she looked like a little child, and we both felt like her mother rather than her student.

When she finally did get out, she was completely rested and I felt that her life force was restored. I felt fortunate for having had that time with her, but was glad for her that she could go back home. I knew our time was close, but I was hoping that we would have another eleven months. I knew from my dream that it would be within a year of the first snow fall. But we had a lot of work to do and three more seminars to go.

I quickly put the dream out of my mind and concentrated on the tasks at hand.

The next seminar was in Toronto, Canada.

In Route to the Toronto Seminar

It had been arranged that I would meet up with Hanna in Chicago, and we would both take the same flight up to Canada. I arrived, weak and shaken, in Chicago after the short flight from Madison. I had picked up something a week earlier, and I was still not completely recovered. It was a weakness that came and went. I noticed it much more once in the airport in Chicago, and I dragged myself over to the phone booth to call Lee.

"Lee, it's Ginger, I'm in Chicago, on my way to Canada. I am going to meet up with Hanna in a few minutes. But Lee, I feel so weak. Something is not right, I don't know what it is. Can you work on me?"

"Sure," Lee said, "I'll do it right away. You will be all right."

"Thanks," I said, and hung up the phone.

I knew she would send me some good energy. I knew she would pray for me. I knew she would do what she could. I was so shaky, I just didn't want to faint or die.

I got down to the gate. The corridors in O'Hare go on forever, and our gate was at the very end. It was packed with people everywhere. I spotted Hanna. She was seated amongst a group of travelers. She was hunched over a book, and as I approached I could see that she had been working on her sermon for her church service on Sunday. But for now, she had dozed off.

When I walked up to her, she began to come out of her sleepy state. At first when she looked up at me, she didn't seem to recognize me. Things must have seemed fuzzy to her. As soon as she knew it was me, she said, "Oh, Ginger, it is you. Can I get you something? Do you need something to eat?"

Now, forgive me, but this seemed bizarre to me. This eighty-four-year old exhausted and sleepy woman's first thought is to take care of me, when I am here to take care of her.

For a moment I was entertaining a funny thought. I thought, "Well yes, Hanna, how about running down that long, long corridor and getting me a hot dog. I'm hungry!"

Of course, I didn't say that.

Anyway, we sat and visited, and then it occurred to me that the Toronto sign was no longer appearing on the gate.

I got up. It was so crowded. I tried to find someone to ask but it was so busy so I went over to the television monitors to confirm, again, that we were at the right gate. I looked at the time, and our flight was scheduled to leave in twenty-five minutes. Scanning the monitor, it became apparent that the gate for our departure flight had been changed to a gate completely across the airport.

I grabbed one of those rolling rental carts. We threw our carry-on luggage onto this cart, and we started running. Hanna was holding onto the cart. When we got to the moving sidewalk, she got on it and walked fast while I ran alongside the walkway with the cart. Then she got off and walked briskly with the aid of the cart to the next moving sidewalk. Again and again, we repeated this procedure.

I could not believe that we had to go clear across the airport. We must have needed the run. It sure woke us both up. We made it just in time. I fell into the seat. I was still shaky. I didn't want Hanna to know that I was puny. I came to help her not to have to get her to help me.

"You sit by the window," Hanna said.

"No, Hanna, you. I don't really care about sitting by the window, and I know you love to," I said.

"No, you sit by the window, so you can see the big lakes," Hanna insisted.

"Okay."

It was no use.

"Just sit down, Ginger," I said to myself. "Look out the window. See the big lakes. Just sit down. Do what she tells you. But I am here to help her, and she loves the window seat."

I heard myself complain, but I sat down and looked out the window anyway.

We didn't talk much. I tried to be quiet to let her get her work done and to get some rest for my shaky and weak body. I noticed that she kept looking over at me.

As we were landing, she started to take off her sweater.

"Here, put this on," she was saying as she was pulling her arms out of the sleeve.

"No, Hanna, I have a jacket."

I motioned to my carry-on bag beneath my feet.

"Put it on," she insisted.

"But Hanna, I am not cold. I'm hot."

The plane was now on the ground, and she was standing at her seat. She was throwing a body block on me. She was not going to let me out without me putting on my jacket. The airplane door had not yet opened, and all the passengers were standing and crowding in the aisles, making it even hotter. Still, she looked at me.

"Okay," I surrendered.

I put my jacket on. I hoped that I would not faint from the heat. She gave me her knapsack to carry. In it she had five sets of five magnets. Each magnet was 450 gauss. I carried the knapsack on my back so, in effect, what was happening was that I was getting an intense magnetic treatment up and down my spine.

Getting Through Customs

We got detained in customs. Apparently the Canadian government frowns on folks who don't know the name of the place they are going to do a lecture. Also, I'm sure Hanna looked suspicious. She came here to present a seminar? She's in her mid eighties. Na.

It didn't help things that Hanna had a short fuse for being detained by anybody or anything. I was not prepared to be a good backup. We flunked the first test—or rather, Hanna did. They sent her to another room. She was supposed to wait in a long, long line. There were no chairs, and there was no one behind those counters who looked like they cared if we got out of there in the next twenty-four hours. There were about fifty people ahead of Hanna.

I told her that I would stand in line for her. She found herself a chair in the customs area. No one told her to move but it was apparently a chair for one of the guards. It surely was not meant for the folks in line.

I was still carrying the knapsack. I was still very weak, and I was still hoping she would not notice. I had to keep squatting so that I wouldn't fall down. The line was creeping, and the clock was ticking. We had a seminar in a few hours, and each minute that we stayed at that airport meant less time for rest and food before the event.

A half an hour became one hour, and now another half an hour. Hanna had enough and now she was going to escape. There were only three more people in front of me. I saw Hanna make her way out of the door toward the outside. I couldn't help myself. I was pleading to her out loud, although I was sure she could not hear me. She was too far away, "No, Hanna, don't do it! Oh, God. Hanna, please don't do it. They are going to catch you. Come back. Don't go through that door. Oh, God, she went through the door."

The people around me were looking at me. They felt bad for me, even if they didn't exactly understand what I was saying. I could see the compassionate looks on the sea of faces. Not too many people in that line spoke English. But they had all watched Hanna's escape attempt.

I didn't know what was going to happen. I had already figured out that the guards and the customs officers had no sense of humor or urgency.

Apparently one of them did have some compassion, since he escorted her back to our side and not to jail. I was so relieved when I saw her come back in.

We finally made it to the counter, and I was ready with the right answers. I didn't know where the event was. Since the seminar sponsor was coming to pick us up and take us there, we thought we really didn't need to know. But I had already figured out that customs did not want that answer. I had pulled out my company newsletter with the schedule printed on it and figured that the name of the hotel where the accommodations were sounded like a reasonable place for a seminar. Apparently, customs thought so too.

They did not like the response that I was simply accompanying her without officially being in her employment, so I decided to let Hanna know that I actually did work for her and she was glad to know that, as was the customs agent.

We were fortunate that the seminar sponsor was still waiting for us when we came out, almost two hours late.

We had no time for anything except to put our luggage in our room and to spend about five minutes freshening up.

The first part of the seminar was with a group of practitioners and advanced students. It was in a small room. It was completely filled.

Hanna went to work. She was excited. A woman had brought in a hydrocephalic child (water head). The child had a shunt placed for drainage. She had also just been tested by the doctors for developmental skills and was assessed as slow and behind in motor and other skills. The baby was not able to do simple things, such as grasp objects.

Hanna took the child and said to the mother, "Well, I'm sorry but that shunt is not in the right place. It is not doing the baby any good."

"Oh, God," I was thinking. "Couldn't we warm up to the group first? Do you have to come out swinging with clubs?"

I knew where Hanna was going with this. She was going to do a hands-on procedure on the baby to relieve the pressure in the head. I had seen this procedure and had done it many times and I knew that it worked, but I had not seen it done on a child who had the shunt "in the wrong place." I was scrambling to get the salt and plastic glove needed for the procedure. I had participated in this with Hanna a number of times.

All of a sudden, I noticed that I was completely healed myself. I was well. No more weakness, no more shakiness. I felt great.

Anyway, Hanna and I did the procedure. It worked. Within thirty minutes the child was grasping the mother's hair and key ring and all the things that baby could not do just a day before when tested.

K.C. and Judy

The next day was the main seminar. It was packed with about two hundred people, almost none of whom I had ever seen, except, K.C. and Judy. I had seen this couple in many of Hanna's seminars in the United States and had subsequently become friends of theirs. They were residents of Canada who spent the winters in Florida.

I remembered meeting them the first time. They had come to Florida to spend their last winter together since K.C. had terminal lung cancer and was told that he would not live another year. He and Judy had spent his supposed last Christmas with their children and were going to Florida to end his life in the warmth of the Florida sun.

Judy, a retired nurse, came to one of the classes I was teaching. K.C. wanted nothing to do with us. He wouldn't even come into our building. He sat for hours in the parking lot waiting for Judy. The only reason that I knew he was there was because his cough was so bad, I could hear it inside the building. It sounded like he was going to cough up his lungs. It was loud, painful sounding, and incessant.

On this fateful and beautiful cool day, we had the doors and windows open in the building to let in the purifying breeze. We had a delightful class, and Judy was leaving with a skip in her step. She was so enthusiastic. She was walking briskly out of the door and suddenly walked right through the screen door, popping it off the track. She was horrified and tickled at the same time. "How absentminded," she said of herself.

God works in strange and effective ways.

In the building came K.C., the gentleman. If his wife had damaged something in our office, he would fix it. He did. And we fixed him. As soon as he entered the building, his coughing began again and when he whipped out his inhaler, I whipped out a natural remedy, peppermint oil.

"This is how we do it," I said to him.

I put a drop of peppermint oil on the back of my hand and licked it.

"This will open the bronchi, immediately."

Now I felt like Hanna!

He did it and it worked. Now I had his attention. We got to work with herbal remedies, homeopathics, and hands-on healing techniques. He started feeling better right away, but it was a slow climb back to health.

Soon after this first meeting, Judy and K.C. came to Hanna's seminar in New Orleans. Right before the seminar was to start, K.C. started with one of his coughing spells. Hanna went over to him. It was very serious. I noticed that Hanna had squeezed down a row of pews and was really working hard on him. I went over to them, and she commanded me to assist her immediately.

"Put your hands here," she said to me as she positioned my hands at his heart and on his upper back.

She reached into her pocket and got out the little brown cubes, the ones like she had used on me when she determined I had a dark force possession. She put those cubes on him and motioned for Lee to come and assist us. At the same time, she kept yelling "Silver, silver!" to LaRae.

LaRae rushed off to get the Colloidal Silver homeopathic.

I had never seen Hanna work so hard. I knew that K.C. might die right there in the pew. This was that critical. But Hanna called Jesus instead of 911. She got K.C. stabilized and then had him come up to the stage. She told the class that we all needed to help to heal this sick man right now. K.C. had this cancer for a long time, and his skin color was gray and skin tone was drawn.

Hanna told us that Jesus used the word "shin" to heal the lepers and that we were going to use it to heal K.C. She directed the group and told us that we were all to say the word very loud three times, pause, and repeat two more times.

K.C. sat on the stage facing the large audience. Hanna put the fingertips of her left hand over his heart and the fingertips of her right hand on his upper back, on his left side. (So that if his body were not in the middle, the finger tips of both of her hands would be touching each other). I had my hands over Hanna's. Together she led the group as we focused our minds and directed the power of the spoken word toward K.C., "Shin! Shin! Shin!"

"Again," Hanna said to us all.

"Shin! Shin! Shin!" we all said as forcefully as we could.

"Again," Hanna directed us.

"Shin! Shin! Shin!" we shouted even more forcefully.

What an amazing moment followed. A gray cloud-like energy lifted from K.C.'s body and a beautiful golden color came into him from the top down. As the gold came in from his crown, the gray moved downward and out until it totally disappeared. He was healed. It was a miracle. He had his life back, and we had witnessed a miracle of God.

Hanna told him that he would still have plenty of work to do to rebuild his body, as it had gotten so weak. He agreed to follow all of her instructions, including the continuation of his herbal program for cleansing the body. Then, he would need to work diligently to rebuild.

That was the first night in years that he slept without coughing.

It was no wonder that this couple followed Hanna wherever they could. She had saved his life. Of course, she gave all the credit to God, as every true healer does.

At the start of the second day of the seminar, Hanna acknowledged that she knew how difficult it was to follow all of the teachings. She said, "Not all of us can do everything right, like Ginger."

This surprised and comforted me and will always remain a sweet memory in my heart. I didn't have a name tag on and no one there except Judy and K.C. Nyland knew my name, so Hanna was saying that just for me. All these years of pushing me and forcing me to be strong, and here she was, at the end of her life, giving me another message that I needed to know. She was telling me that I had done a good job. She was acknowledging that I had listened to her teachings. I was living them, and she noticed. I felt a glow in my own heart. I never needed to hear her say those words, but I cherished the energy behind them as much then as I do now.

Chapter 17

A New Beginning

Teaching with Hanna

During her stay with me in October, it was decided that I would assist her at all of her five-day seminars at her retreat center in Boulder for the next summer season. This came about very oddly. We had been sitting at my dining room table when she looked me squarely in the eye and, in her high-pitched voice and animated ways, said, "I am looking and looking and looking for someone to help me teach at my summer retreat."

At this point, I had been "on the road" teaching Hanna's work for about seven years. I knew that Hanna was well aware of this fact, as well as the fact that I had assisted her with seminars and trade shows all over the place. Anyhow, I figured she wasn't talking about me. If she wanted me to come to Boulder, she would just ask. So, I didn't say anything to her. I just looked at her and nodded. I took it as a share.

The next day it happened again. When we were sitting at the table and she said, "I am looking and looking and looking for someone to come help me with my retreat."

This time I thought, "What am I, chopped liver?"

Later that day, LaRae, Hanna, and I were all seated at the table when the same subject came up, "I am looking and looking and looking for someone to help me with my retreat."

LaRae and I looked at each other from across the table. Telecommunication was occurring. Silently, I beseeched her to tell me if I should say something to Hanna. I mean, should I be so bold? Would she say, "No, I don't mean you"?

I could read LaRae's mind. "Say it," she was telling me.

So I just blurted it out.

"Well, Hanna, if you need someone to help you teach your school, I will do it. I would love to come to Boulder to teach, but I didn't think you were talking about me."

"Oh, good!" she said, and she was glad I would be with her.

By the end of the day, we had our whole schedule for teaching together planned. We had also agreed to extend the time for the combined Level 1 & 2 classes to five days, for which I would fly to Boulder to help her. We scheduled eight of the five-day formats, and we shaved the regular Level 1 & 2s down to three days, a format that she felt she had the energy to teach alone or with a few guest speakers.

We had it all set. We were both excited and relieved, and I was honored by the opportunity that was being presented to me.

The Summer Retreat Begins, First Week of May 1998

As the time drew near, I felt confident that God had given Hanna an extension on her life as she had already taught one class, and she was still alive. Surely if God gave her to us that long, He was going to let us have her for another summer. Then I would be more ready and more able to handle the tasks that lay ahead of me.

Hanna Passes

I arrived in Boulder on the afternoon of Wednesday, May 6, two days before the start of the second class. I had come to back Hanna up for the weekend, although it was not a class I was scheduled to teach. I wanted time to get organized for the summer, for the eight classes for which I was scheduled.

I kept thinking that I should go over to Hanna's Wednesday afternoon, but for some reason I didn't. Early evening, I went to dinner with her business manager, Tom Brown, his wife, and son, instead of going over to Hanna's. When leaving the restaurant, Tom asked me what was on my agenda for the next few days, and I said, "Nothing. I don't even know why I am here this early."

We laughed, and I went to check into a hotel.

The next morning, bright and early, I got ready, had a good breakfast, and almost skipped taking my herbs—except I was sure I heard Hanna say, "Take your supplements." I went back and got them and took them and headed to her home. It was always so exciting for me to go down that dusty, bumpy road to her home at Peaceful Meadow Retreat. As I was driving slowly on her road, I saw someone waving to me in my rearview mirror. I stopped the car and jumped out, happily, to greet Tom Brown.

What a beautiful, sunny, clear morning it was in the foothills of Boulder, Colorado. Tom gently took me by the shoulders and said something foreign like, "Oh, you haven't heard?"

I made some stupid joke about what I might have heard. But Tom wasn't laughing.

"Hanna passed away this morning."

"You're joking," I kept repeating. But looking into his eyes, I finally absorbed the message. It sunk in that Hanna's death was not something he would joke about. "What happened?" I asked Tom.

"Klaus (Hanna's son) went in to get her for morning chapel at 6 A.M., and she was still alive. When she didn't get up, he went back to get her at 7 o'clock," he said. "She was gone. Apparently in peace, she had a beautiful smile on her face."

Tom looked at me, as I stared at the Rocky Mountains, I supposed expecting me to cry.

"Are you okay?" Tom asked.

I said, "Yes, we knew this would happen someday." Nothing could have prepared us for the loss. We could never have told God we were ready to lose Hanna. But we had prepared ourselves for the work we would need to face when Hanna passed, and now was the time.

I took the rest of the road to Hanna's. I went into the grief of her family and her employees. I went into her bedroom, where her body lay so peacefully under the blankets, and I saw that she was in tremendous peace.

Vicki Opfer was kneeling by her side when her grandson showed me into her room. John Demaray had already placed the red rose on her chest

153

as Hanna had always told us to do when a person passes. Someone else had lit a candle. Carol Ostroff had arrived from California for the class only hours after Hanna's passing. She brought with her a beautiful little heart-shaped dried flower arrangement that she had made for Hanna. A little later in the morning, this was placed on Hanna's feet.

I knelt down by her head, stroked her hair and kissed her face. I knew my life had just changed again and forever. Gone was the person who had originally made God so available to me, gone from the physical body and no longer just a phone call away. I could feel the aching in my own soul, and I wanted to remember the holy, sacred feeling of these moments with her.

I wanted to remember everything she had ever taught me. I wanted to do what she wanted me to do, but most of all I wanted to take yesterday back and have come here to be with her and have one more time with her and have her say one more thing to me. Instead, I had gone to the hotel and slept twelve hours, an unusual thing for me to do. I wanted to take Wednesday back, if only I could.

Visitation

I left and entered her tiny room many times that day. During one visitation, I noticed that someone had placed a freshly picked bouquet of tulips on her chest. Vicki said her son, Heinz, placed it there. I took in the tenderness of this action, and my heart ached. I was glad I had work to do.

There Hanna lay for the rest of the day, as the family and a few of her congregation and students went by her side and spoke to her and prayed. Linda Demaray, a dear friend of Hanna's, with her husband and their three adult children, John, David, and Cindy joined Vicki by staying the whole day in vigil by her bedside. I was glad that they stayed. I had things to do now. There was much work to be done, but it was fitting that these few beloved ones should stay in vigil with her body.

Over the next few days, joined by members of Hanna's congregation, we all prepared her home and retreat center for the crowds that were sure to show up for her memorial on Sunday.

Linda and Vicki did most of the organization for the memorial services, and the rest of us concentrated on getting the house in order.

Hanna's step-grandchildren and her daughter-in-law, Martha, worked with reverence behind the scenes to make everything nice. Anna and Martha began cleaning Hanna's quarters immediately and continued until it was indeed neat and fitting for a saint to rest. (Hanna never allowed anyone to help her with those chores when she was alive).

José

Throughout the next few days, the sound of a saw cutting wood accompanied our grief and chores, as José Martinez (another of Hanna's step grandchildren) and José Alvarado (his friend) worked to build the stand for Hanna's coffin. After the stand was finished, José (Hose A) and José (Hose B) as they affectionately referred to themselves, continued to cut. They cut the branches off trees, trimmed bushes, cut grass and anything else in their path.

José had planted a row of willow trees years ago when he was a young boy. Now they were in need of care, and José needed to cut them. He seemed to work his grief out on the land and the projects. He was silent and steady, working day and night, fixing and building and grooming, all for his Hanna and his heart. Sometimes our eyes would meet. No words were necessary.

Getting Ready

In the middle of all of this, the phone was ringing incessantly as people began to hear the news. Some people had not heard but were calling to register for her summer retreat. Surely the summer classes at the retreat would be canceled. No Hanna, no retreat. This was too obvious.

After sitting in Tom Brown's office with some of Hanna's key employees along with Alberto, her retreat manager and grandson, we all agreed that Hanna would want us to continue the retreats. I agreed to run the retreat as "Director of Education" with two stipulations. The first stipulation was that I had complete control over who the other teachers would be. I had learned from the past and I did not want to end up having to battle others for the way that I knew Hanna wanted things to be taught. The other agreement that I insisted on was that Alberto Kroeger would have total control over the operations of the retreat center meaning that his authority would not be "usurped" by anyone for any reason. This was the only way it would really work for us and for the retreat, in light of everything. Everyone agreed, and we went forward.

We were not sure if anyone would still want to come to the retreat, but the phone kept ringing. Many people seemed more determined than ever to get to the retreat to learn the work. Others seemed to be driven by the desire to make a spiritual pilgrimage to the house of this holy being, a true servant of God. Some just wanted to be in her energy field, which is still so palpable. So, we felt it was the right decision.

Her memorial service on Sunday was beautiful. José and José had wired the chapel and the overflow rooms for sound to accommodate the large number in attendance.

During this time there were twelve who stayed for the services who had shown up thinking they were there to attend a class. Phyllis, Betty, Marijan, and a few others had taken special care to insure that the memorial areas were beautified with large photos of Hanna that were placed amid bouquets of flowers and candles which graced tables draped with linens. Carol H. ran the kitchen. And with the help from Mary Ellen, Richard, Joan, Frank, Milo, Beth, Rose, Bo, Wynell, Linda, Holly, Jean Marie, Jeannie, Lois and Richard G., Irma and others, everything got done in time.

As the people arrived, the energy of the event and the day enveloped us all. The angelic beings were there; we could feel their presence.

Tuesday's memorial service was at a mortuary in town and open to the public. The place was filled with hundreds of people, and we again said our good-byes and remembrances of our dear Hanna.

When the memorial services were over, it was time to prepare the retreat center for the upcoming class. Three days later, the class began to arrive, and on Friday night we officially began the first retreat class without Hanna's physical presence. What a fabulous group of students showed up for that class! Certainly Hanna had hand picked them all.

Alberto

Alberto Kroeger was amazing. Hanna, his grandmother, his employer, and best friend, had just died. Yet he found the strength, between tears, to call every one of the 600 people who were registered for classes to let them know of Hanna's passing and to encourage them to come anyway.

I was empowered by him. I felt so supported. I had agreed to do the teaching, and at the time I didn't know if I would have any other teachers to help me.

Ever since he was a young boy, Alberto and I had shared a special bond. Now we knew why. We had work to do together. We clung to each other for strength and support.

The Teachers

I was fortunate to be joined quickly by three other teachers to help me teach the summer classes—Bobbi Brooks, Milo Beaver, and Beth Hedstrom. We all pulled together. We had an instant love and admiration for each other and for teaching which grew more each day.

We are committed to the continuation of Hanna's teachings and to supporting others who want to learn and teach the work. So much help is needed in this world.

Gisela

I had always known that Hanna had a daughter who lived in Connecticut, but I had never met her. I understood from Hanna that Gisela was not interested in Hanna's work. She was living her own life far from the crowds around Hanna. On some level, I could actually understand that. Hanna didn't seem to have a "personal life." She had sacrificed her life to the world community, one person at a time. Even though I didn't travel or work nearly as much as Hanna, I was already finding it hard to squeeze in personal time and vacation time. There were some years that vacations just didn't happen.

The day that Hanna passed, Gisela arrived, as did her cousins and a brother from California along with many others. There was a hub of activity in the house as we each seemed to get lost in the endless tasks that needed to be done.

I instantly felt a kinship with Gisela. She had so much of Hanna's energy and enthusiasm. She was warm and loving and, unlike Hanna, liked to hug. We needed lots of hugs during the next few months. She always had her arms open. Her presence and the ways that she reminded us all of Hanna made it easier for us to get through those initial months after Hanna's passing.

Other Dreams/Other Healers

My relationship with Hanna had given me an unquenchable thirst for healing techniques and interactions of all kinds with the Divine. Throughout the years this thirst had led me to many things and many people, even in my dream state. There were a number of holy people and healers that I still wanted to meet, and now they were dying one by one. Harvey had passed on a few years earlier. Dr. Fulford, a ninety-five year old osteopath with the gift of healing, had just passed. Prior to Hanna's passing, knowing it was coming soon, I began to get the feeling that I should take the time out to meet some of them, before it was too late.

Mother Theresa

A few days prior to Mother Theresa's passing, I dreamed of running in to her in an airport. "Oh Mother Theresa!" I exclaimed. "You are the person I most wanted to meet in the world."

She and a few of the nuns accompanying her stopped and listened to me with polite regard. She took my face in her hands and touched her forehead to mine. Each time she did this, I would bend all the way back, unlike my Mother whose body stayed straight and firm when Mother Theresa did this to her.

I wished I could stay firm like my mother. Why was I bending all the way back into a back bend? Later I realized, oh, this is okay. Mama is firm in her beliefs and her religion, and I am flexible in my beliefs and in my spiritual life. We are each different, but this is not a problem. Mother Theresa was not bothered by it. Why should I be?

Then she told me that she was going to give me the power to heal others. At that point she shot a little red bullet out of her eye toward mine. My reaction was to dodge the bullet. It was such a sudden action and reaction. I instantly knew that I shouldn't have jumped out of the way. Fortunately, she did it again, and this time I allowed it in my eye. Now I had the power to heal others.

I awoke from the dream with no evidence of having some new power or method to heal. However, I now had a burning desire to meet Mother Theresa. I dropped a note to my sister Mercedes.

"Please find out where Mother Theresa is, and let's go meet her," I wrote. I didn't care where we had to go, and I knew Mercedes could find out where she was and could also afford to go with me.

Mother Theresa died before my sister got the letter. I cried.

A Dream of a Healing

Some years earlier I had dreamed that Hanna was ill, and one of these TV Evangelists was going to try to heal her. Hanna was in a big gymnasium with many others, and I was viewing this all from a one-way mirror with my angel. The minister laid his hands on Hanna and healed her and then proceeded to try to explain how the whole thing worked. I was flabbergasted at how bogus his explanation was of how the healing had occurred.

The angel said to me, "You see, it doesn't matter that he doesn't know how the healing really occurred because all healing comes from God anyway. She is healed. The minister played his part, and he does believe. He is not accurate about how it happens, but she is healed, and that's all that matters."

Okeeey dookeey, now I was going to have to give up a prejudice even I didn't know I had, against TV Evangelists. I can't even catch a break in my sleep!

Jesus in My Dreams

On a number of occasions, I had a visit from Jesus in my dreams. Once he came because for six months I had been suffering with a sciatica type pain in my hip. It was getting worse. At first I thought it was due to working out some muscular cobwebs with the hatha yoga exercises that I was doing. When those exercises and various herbal and homeopathic remedies that should have worked didn't, I was lost.

Jesus paid me a sweet little visit and very matter-of-factly said, "You have a urinary tract infection. Drink cranberry juice." The next day I went to the health food store and bought the good cranberry juice concentrate, went home, and mixed myself my first glass. I continued to sip on some for the next few days, but within a few hours the condition that had dragged out for so long was completely cleared. (I guess Jesus knows what He's talking about!)

In another dream that I had, some of my peers and I were hosting a parade for Jesus. We were all very excited and had told many people to show up and get a hug from Jesus. I knew that hundreds would believe us and would come. Others would think we were wacky and would stay away.

When Jesus arrived he hugged each of us (the parade organizers). When I looked out to see the crowd that had shown up for the parade, I saw hundreds of thousands of people. I realized that there were too many people for Jesus to actually be able to give each a personal hug, and I felt sad. I didn't just want a hug for me; I wanted them to have a hug too. But I knew that they would get many blessings from His mere presence, and so it was.

Jesus turned to the group of us and said, "You are the original pioneers." He thanked us for our work and dedication to it against many adversities. Yes, it was true. We were pioneers. There were many, many times that people ridiculed us and threatened us. Laws and regulations were written to keep us from helping, healing or touching people. Hanna and her cronies had it much worse. Hanna was indicted a number of times for practicing medicine without a license and was even "found guilty of healing a person." Not guilty of *trying* to heal someone, she was found

159

guilty of *actually healing* someone.

Jesus gave us the command to "help one another and to heal others." He did not give us the command to go to medical school. In the meantime, we have become ministers with a healing ministry. Ministers can lay hands on people. That's how we do it without running afoul of the law.

So yes, we are pioneers forging a new frontier in the realm of human consciousness. This new awareness is that we are able to make a difference—each one of us. We can understand health and healing on all levels and we can learn to help ourselves and to help each other.

I Met Dr. Fuller in My Dreams

About two years prior to Hanna's passing I had a very powerful and mystifying dream. Being the New Orleans native that I am, I seem to have "parades" in my dreams a good deal. This time we were having a parade, but I couldn't remember for whom. Before the parade started I was standing on the side of the road waiting. Down the center of the road came a lone elderly man with white beard and snow white hair. His coat was of a strange multicolored quilted pattern. Surely he was not from our time. His clothes were from another period in history.

All of a sudden a force came from behind me and made me bow with reverence at his feet. I tried to resist the force but there I was in the center of the road bowing to this holy man. Who was he? I had to know. I had to find him. I awoke from the dream.

This dream and this man's presence followed me around for days. Who was he? How could I find out? Was he Moses? Was he a Christian saint or an Indian saint? I searched in books and photos. I could find people who looked similar but they were not the man I saw. How could I find this man? I was supposed to find him and learn from him, this I was sure. I would have to be given more instructions because no one seemed to have any idea who he could be.

I had to put this search on the back burner until I had more clues.

As time went on, I heard of this elderly minister, Dr. Willard Fuller, who had quite a reputation as a healer but was particularly known for his dental healings.

Through Dr. Hulda Clark's teachings, I understood that although you can help someone heal from all kinds of illnesses, if you have an underlying problem in the teeth and the jaw bones (which often goes undetected), you are fighting a losing battle.

I often wondered about those people that got well and then got sick again and got well and slid back. These, I found out, were often the ones with dental issues. If there was someone who could heal teeth, I needed to find him and try to get my dental problems healed and also learn the work.

My travel schedule was crammed. There was not an available weekend for me to attend one of his healing meetings, and I so wanted to experience one of them. On my way back from Syracuse, New York, I was finally going to get to meet him. He was scheduled to have a healing service at the Unity Church in Detroit. The first leg of my flight was from Syracuse to Detroit, and the second leg was from Detroit to Madison. I arranged to have a four-hour layover in Detroit.

My friend Mary, who lived in Michigan, picked me up at the Detroit airport, and we scooted over to the church. I was excited.

Dr. Fuller, a tall elderly man with stark white hair and a white beard was dressed in a handsome black suit. Throughout the service we sang and listened to his funny stories. I could feel the energy of enthusiasm increasing in me and in the rest of the group.

I was smiling and leaning forward, trying to take in every word he said. As is usual for me, I found myself mesmerized by his words and his love for the work. As I was gazing intently at him I suddenly saw him fade into the huge quilted backdrop against the wall behind the alter. It was a bright, multicolored, quilted pattern, and it enveloped him.

"Oh my God! The jacket! The dream! It was you. You were the holy man that I was supposed to find, and here you are. I have found you, the man of my dreams!"

As I was having this revelation I sat up straight and must have had a shocked look on my face. Of course I didn't say a word, there was a church full of people there. But as I was remembering the dream and realizing who he was, he turned to me and looked me right in the eye. He smiled and nodded his head as if to say, "Yes! I am the one in the dream."

When it was time for the laying-on of hands section, I was so nervous and excited that my stomach was lurching. Then Dr. Fuller announced that he would lay hands-on the people on the opposite side of the church from Mary and me. His wife, Althea, would lay hands-on our side of the church. I was so crest fallen. She seemed like a nice woman but he was the one with the gift. I wanted him. I tried to be a "big girl" while going through the line, and I hoped my disappointment wouldn't scream into Althea's face.

When Althea touched me on the face, I felt the energy. She was a conduit as well as Dr. Fuller. I had the most incredible experience of peace wash over me along with an understanding that entered my heart. The energy that was pouring through me was not coming from Althea nor would it have come from Dr. Fuller. It was the energy of God, and they were standing in that Divine vortex calling it in with enough faith and love that it actually transmitted to each one of us.

After this section Dr. Fuller looked into many mouths to see if there were healings taking place. Of course he hadn't looked into anyone's mouth prior to the event, so he would ask the person about their dental health prior to the touch (most people are well aware if they are missing teeth or if they have any gold or silver fillings). Then he would examine their mouth and literally watch the healing occur. He said that often other kinds of healing took place within the body, but dental healings were the ones that we could easily see. We couldn't see if someone was healed of leukemia.

Each of us looked into our own mouths with dental mirrors and hand-held mirrors. Many people were seeing changes as their mercury or silver fillings turned to a bright, shiny gold or filled in with a white substance.

I was gazing into a woman's mouth as I watched one of her teeth growing back. I talked to another woman who claimed that all of her mercury fillings had turned to gold. I marveled at these apparent miracles. I kept looking into my mouth hoping to see new teeth pop out at a few extraction sites where my root canal teeth had been, but I did not have this kind of healing. However, my bite, which had bothered me ever since I started getting my mercury amalgam fillings removed was corrected instantly.

The seminar continued and then ended, and I was in bliss. There were crowds around Dr. Fuller, and I only got to speak with him for a moment. It was time for Mary to take me to the airport for the last leg of my trip back to Madison. So, we went.

I made the commitment to learn from him as soon as possible. But then I got busy, and before I knew it I was going to teach with Hanna at the retreat. Then Hanna died, and things got really hectic.

The first summer after Hanna's passing, I commuted from Boulder to Madison. I had a business in Madison so I had to travel back and forth. Now that Hanna had passed it made me even more aware how precious time is and how much there is to learn. I wanted so much to learn Dr.

Fuller's work, but how? My schedule was now booked until the end of the year since I had taken on Hanna's teaching schedule in addition to my own.

Dr. Fuller kept popping up in my consciousness, but I had to keep telling him to go away. "Not now, I don't have time." I would say to myself when I thought of needing to study with him.

Finally, I surrendered to the process. While sitting in my office in Madison, I decided to give him a call and see if he was going to be anywhere close to Boulder during the summer school season. If so, he could come and give us a three hour healing meeting. I didn't even know if he was even in the country when I made the call. I was well aware that he traveled internationally with his ministry. But, I took a chance anyway, knowing that I could leave a message for him and at least get the ball rolling.

He answered the phone. By the time we got off the line an hour later we had him scheduled to come to the retreat to do a healing meeting and to teach all three levels of his seminar. All those attending every hour of the three seminars would then be ordained into a healing ministry. All of this could happen as long as the plan with the group in Venezuela fell through.

I prayed, "God bless Venezuela, and give them a better date for the seminar. Their date is the only one that works for us, so, God, bless them and give us their time slot!"

Sure enough, we got him for that time.

Dr. Fuller came and taught us. It was a wonderful seminar and a mystical event. He was able to facilitate the descent of the Holy Spirit for each of us. This filled and empowered us with divine energy. He taught us that we were able to call on this energy.

I had known for many years that we had the Divine right and the command from Jesus to help and to heal others. Now I understand what Hanna was accessing when she called on the power of God and then healed someone. It is the energy, the energy of the Holy Spirit. It is available to each of us through the power of faith.

Listening and Communicating

None of us will ever be able to take Hanna's, Dr. Fuller's, Harvey Bevier's, Mother Theresa's or any other healer's place. We each have to work with ourselves, building on our own understanding of our gifts and take the work of helping others out to the world in our own way.

My understanding has continued to expand, as has my reverence for God, Jesus, and all beings. I went in pursuit of understanding energy as an intellectual endeavor only to discover that it is not something that can be understood with the head alone. This understanding must come through the higher intelligence of the heart. To understand energy, we have to know that we are all part of the One Spirit. Our spiritual self is not separate from our physical reality, even if we are unaware of this. We are spiritual beings with a soul, a body, and a personal identity. We are forever in the heart of God, regardless of our faults, flaws, mistakes, accomplishments, or lack of understanding.

Going Home

After two summers of teaching in Boulder, I got the message that it was time to focus my energy on my business, my family, and some of the creative projects that I had been wanting to do. I needed to go back to learning and studying with a limited teaching schedule. I needed to stay home in Madison and regenerate my own life force. This freed up my personal energy and allowed me time to focus on what I thought God wanted me to do. I felt compelled to put some of these stories down and to do some other projects. I needed to stretch my wings again.

Now Chris and I Can Finally Write Another Song

So, after all of this, my friend Chris (who had spent some time around the retreat with me since Hanna's passing) and I wrote this song. It was a long time coming. We had wandered halfway around the world, both separately and together, trying to understand life. Now we finally had something to write about.

I understand on a much deeper level now about "listening and communicating with energy." Energy is something I now have a personal relationship with. I have experienced that God is the Ultimate of all energies and is a part of us in each moment, in every hour and in every breath we take. We are never alone.

We have each been given a mission, which is up to us to fulfill. We are to love ourselves and, with this love, help and love each other. We have the ability to make a difference in this world through our goodness and our light.

So arriving at that understanding, Chris and I wrote this song:

Energy

A Song to God

"Energy"— A Song to God

There you are
always next to me
and there's a feel in the air
and it's like
an energy
lifting me
to a place where I can see and believe
I believe ...
And I remember times
just praying
that things would work out my way
and I could hear you say
trust the steps along the way
And there you were
always next to me
I can feel you in the air I breathe
and it's like
an energy
lifting me
to a place where I can see and believe
I believe...
And I remember times
just praying
that I would hear what you were saying
for the steps along the way
for every step along the way
And there you were
always next to me
and there's a feel in the air
and it's like
an Energy
lifting me
to a place where I can see
and believe
I believe ...

Many thanks and much love to Dell Frickey for doing the musical notation of "Energy."

Author's Afterward

In 2002, after ten fabulous years, LaRae and I sold Southern Herb Company and moved from our beloved Madison, Wisconsin. In search of new frontiers and a warmer climate, we found ourselves in Ozark, Missouri. When people ask, Why Missouri? we simply answer, We don't know. When we find out, we'll let you know.

In September of 2003, I completed my doctoral programs at both HOLOS University Graduate Seminary and Greenwich University, where my research and my doctoral dissertation was done on the effectiveness of Hanna Kroeger's work.

Through my involvement with QXCI, SCIO, the VIBE machine, research, writing and a continued love for natural foods and nutritional supplements and other new energy medicine products and modalities, Energy Medicine Ministries, Energy Medicine Product Distributors and Energy Medicine Productions were birthed. Our commitment is now, as it has always been, to the health and healing of humanity. Our ministry and our distribution company still stand on the foundation of Hanna Kroger's work in natural and spiritual healing. She will forever be our guiding light.

For more information about
Dr. Bowler's work,
her teaching schedule
and additional books,
please visit us at www.gingerbowler.com

Please visit

or call

Energy Medicine Publishing

Energy Medicine Product Distributors

1.800.240.3211